STANFORD

Portrait of a University

by Susan Wels

Foreword by Gerhard Casper

Stanford Alumni Association
Stanford, California

Holly Brady
Executive Editor

Tom Walker
Art Director

Amy Pilkington
Art and Production Manager

Rod Searcey
Artifact Photographer

Laura Donohue
Copy Editor

Margaret Kimball
University Archivist

Library of Congress Catalog Card Number:
99-070903

ISBN: 0-916318-56-7

Printed in Hong Kong

10 9 8 7 6 5 4 3 2 1

First edition

CONTENTS

HOPE

Foreword

WHEN I FIRST ARRIVED ON THE FARM IN MY NEW ROLE AS PRESIDENT-elect, I was challenged to an "advanced placement history test." Over dinner with a group of faculty, a member of the history department asked me whether I knew Stanford's motto. I had to admit my ignorance.

The next day—having spent the intervening hours educating myself—I was able to recount that Stanford's first president, David Starr Jordan, chose *Die Luft der Freiheit weht* ("The wind of freedom blows") as the University's informal motto. It still can be found in the president's seal. It seemed to me then, as it seems to me now, that Jordan's choice serves as shorthand for principles fundamental to Stanford. It constitutes a statement about freedom of inquiry and reflects a strong element of the challenges that Stanford has embraced.

For a relatively young university, Stanford has a history rich in research and scholarship; in athletic achievements and artistic creativity; in loyalty of alumni and friends; and in contributions to California, the nation, and the world. Similarly, Stanford is rich in "place"—meaning both its location in the American West and the remarkable physical expression of its traditions, as described by Jordan, in the "red-tiled roofs against the azure sky." For alumni, memories of their university clearly include the physical setting and the architecture that make up the campus. Famous landmarks and quiet corners trigger associations that are historical, aesthetic, and personal. Often these landmarks are places to which students feel connected for the rest of their lives.

In these pages, we celebrate the legacy and the sense of "place" that is Stanford. At a true university, those who participate in its life must draw together and jointly reinvent the university every day. Even after 100 years—or, for that matter, 500 years—the days of a university must always be *first* days. The strength of the university cannot be maintained unless it is continuously considered afresh.

Preceding pages: In 1999, the earthquake-damaged Stanford Museum reopened as part of the new Iris & B. Gerald Cantor Center for the Visual Arts; rainbow over campus; mosaic and stonework in the Inner Quad.

To do that, we remember the past, why we are here, and what those before us have achieved. By comparison with some universities, Stanford's history does not seem long. However, what really matters in a university's history are commitment and continuity. Stanford is an institution that has benefited from commitment handed down from one generation of faculty, and one generation of students, to the next. This institution's age is not so much expressed by the number of years of its formal existence, but by the active engagement of faculty, students, staff, trustees, alumni, parents, and friends, their commitment, and the continuity of a tradition.

During his inauguration as Stanford president in 1949, Wally Sterling said this: "I have read something of Stanford's history. It has not been untroubled by adversities and disappointments. But it is essentially the story of strong growth from good soil and, as any person is enhumbled in the presence of greatness, so I am in the knowledge of what has been accomplished here."

A Stanford student recently told me, "It is a gift to be on the Stanford campus. If you do not enjoy some part of it every day, you feel guilty for rejecting a gift." I hope this book will give its readers a sense of that gift.

Gerhard Casper
President, Stanford University

Left: *After many years in storage, this 1899 bronze statue of the Stanford family—originally located in the Quad's Memorial Court—was placed near the family's Mausoleum in 1998.*

THE WIND
OF FREEDOM

Preceding pages: *The rolling hills of Leland and Jane Stanford's Palo Alto farm.*
Left: *Women students pass through the arcades of the Inner Quad. From the beginning, Senator Stanford declared, "I want, in this school, that one sex shall have equal advantages with the other."*

O THOSE WHO LAID EYES ON LELAND STANFORD Junior University for the first time on the brilliant autumn morning of October 1, 1891, the sight must have seemed equally inspired and audacious. In the middle of a dry plain on Senator Stanford's immense Palo Alto farm—nearly 3,000 miles from the centers of culture and learning in the East, and surrounded by open fields and rutted tracks—stood the most imposing architecture ever conceived for an American university. Under a porcelain-blue sky stretched the long, low lines of a massive quadrangle of richly chiseled sandstone, its graceful arcades enclosing a formal open court. According to one New York newspaper, the newborn university appeared to have been conjured "Aladdin-like," amid the rural estate's fields and golden hills.

To the classrooms of this institution came 15 young professors who had traveled "from a distance to a half-discovered country," according to David Starr Jordan, the University's first president. They were a "handful of young idealists, with much less wisdom than enthusiasm." Five hundred fifty-five students arrived, too—more than double the anticipated number. The exuberance of faculty and students was widely shared on that bright October morning, as thousands of wellwishers joined them for the official opening ceremonies. Arriving at the farm on foot, on horseback, by surrey, buggy, and train, the guests streamed into the sun-splashed courtyard, packing it

shoulder to shoulder and crowding the shady sand-stone arcades. Pampas plumes, palmettos, and bright banners fluttered around the Quad's great western arch, and students cheered as Senator Leland and Jane Stanford officially opened the university they had named for their late son. It was, for the two eminent and aging founders, a moment that climaxed years of effort, plans, and dreams. But for the faculty, students, and throngs of supporters who joined them on that blazing Thursday morning, it was only the beginning of great hopes and expectations.

The students, wild and rough by some accounts, came from all across the country. Five journeyed from Japan, and others made their way from Europe and Canada. "Students from everywhere sent inquiries and applications," remembered Ellen Coit Elliot, wife of the University's first registrar, "…for this university was rumored to teach everything…and its scope would be 'from the kindergarten up.' Besides, it was in *California*." Unshackled by conventions, the new University was nonsectarian, tuition-free, and open to all students—men and women, rich and poor, without regard to means or social status.

Academically, as well, Stanford set its course in a bold direction. "If I thought the University was to be only like the others in this country," the senator declared from the beginning, "I had better have given the money to some existing institution. I want it to be on a different plan." Unlike the traditional American college—which required students to take a rigid regimen of Greek, Latin, mathematics, and philosophy—Stanford had no required subjects except English, and individual professors were free to devise their own courses of studies for their students. Moreover, the new University would blend theory with application, cultural education with practical preparation

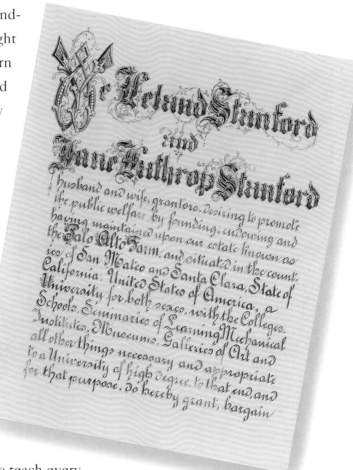

Left: *David Starr Jordan, Stanford's first president, addresses the crowd at the University's opening ceremonies on October 1, 1891.* Above: *The University's Founding Grant, calligraphed on parchment, was signed by Leland and Jane Stanford on November 11, 1885.*

Early Campus Life

WHEN STANFORD FIRST OPENED, 15 professors taught subjects that included chemistry, physics, history, zoology, English, civil engineering, mathematics, physiology, and geology. By the University's fourth year, student enrollment had almost doubled, from 555 in 1891 to 1,101 in 1895.

For transportation around campus and to nearby towns, students and faculty members walked or relied on bicycles and horse-drawn buggies. The first automobile appeared on campus in 1899, but in 1901, Mrs. Stanford banished the dangerous "devil wagons" from University grounds. The ban was lifted in 1914. *Right:* An 1895 football banner.

in the professional fields. Senator Stanford "had no sympathy with the use of the college as a group of social clubs, nor did he wish to train gentlemen of leisure," recalled Jordan, a distinguished ichthyologist and former president of Indiana University. Jordan believed that a Stanford man "should be one who knows something and can carry his knowledge into action." Free from "the dead hands of old traditions" and dedicated to the new and useful, Stanford University would be a place that valued excellence, research, and the scholarly, contemplative life. Hallowed by no traditions and hampered by none, Jordan noted in his opening address, Stanford "has no history to fall back upon…. Its fingerposts," he declared, "all point forward."

For Leland Stanford, establishing the University was the last great effort in a lifetime of prodigious achievements. Born near Albany, New York, in 1824 and educated as a lawyer, Stanford migrated to California in 1852 and prospered by selling provisions in mining camps in the Sierra foothills. After moving to Sacramento with his wife, Jane, in 1855, he immersed himself in politics, helping to organize the state's fledgling Republican party and campaigning vigorously for Lincoln in 1860. The next year, at the age of 37, Stanford was elected governor. During the Civil War, he struggled to keep California in the Union. After the war, he worked to cement physically the bonds between the Union and Pacific states by spearheading construction of the Central Pacific railroad, the western segment of America's first transcontinental rail line. With a silver hammer, Stanford himself drove the gold spike that ceremonially completed the railroad link across the continent at Promontory, Utah, on May 10, 1869.

That achievement was a pinnacle of his professional and political career, and it followed by a year the happiest event of his family life. On May 14, 1868, after 18 years of marriage, Leland and Jane Stanford celebrated the birth of their first and only

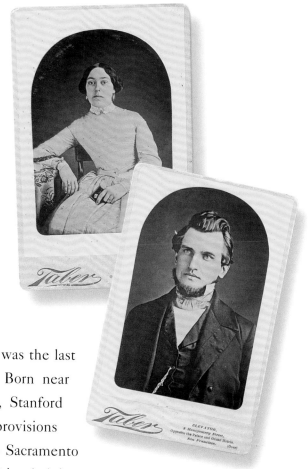

Jane Lathrop and Leland Stanford were married in 1850 in Albany, New York. Five years later, Jane joined Leland in California, where he and his brothers operated stores in mining camps. The couple settled in Sacramento, where the Stanford brothers had a thriving retail business. After serving as governor of California, Stanford headed construction of the Central Pacific Railroad. He was a U.S. senator from 1885 until his death in 1893.
Left: In 1869, Leland Stanford drove the gold spike that completed the nation's first transcontinental rail line.

Leland Stanford Jr at 2 yrs old
Presented by David Oliver Cobo S.F.
when 5yrs of age visited Leland Jr.

Born in 1868, Leland DeWitt
was Leland and Jane Stanford's
only child. As he grew older, he
enjoyed painting, wood carving,
and collecting historical
and archaeological objects.

child, a son they named Leland Dewitt Stanford. According to Jane's secretary and biographer Bertha Berner, the newborn was so adored that one evening in Sacramento his father had him presented to dinner party guests on a silver tray, nestled on a bed of blossoms.

Young Leland grew to be a curious, precocious, and intelligent child fascinated by history, mathematics, and mechanical and handmade objects. Fluent in both French and German, the boy traveled widely with his parents. His admiration for his father was so great that, at the age of nine, Leland Dewitt requested that his name formally be changed to Leland Stanford, Jr.

During the summer and fall of 1883, soon after the youngster turned 15, the Stanfords embarked on an extended trip to England, France, and Germany. The family spent the Christmas holidays in Vienna and then, after the New Year, journeyed on to Constantinople, Greece, and Italy. In Naples, the boy fell ill, but was apparently well enough to press on with his parents to Rome, where the family stopped briefly before going on to Florence. There, young Leland was diagnosed with "a mild case of typhoid fever," a disease he had apparently contracted in Constantinople. He spent three feverish weeks in a darkened room at the Hotel Bristol, toward the end of which he appeared to be recovering. Then suddenly, he took a turn for the worse, and on March 13, 1884, he died, just two months short of his 16th birthday. His father, exhausted and despairing, dreamed on the night of his son's death that young Leland instructed him to carry on, exhorting him to "live for humanity." Stanford told his wife the dream, and they both took it to heart. By the time they arrived in New York in April with their son's body, they had both firmly resolved to found an educational institution in Leland Jr.'s memory. "Since I could do no more for my boy," Stanford confided to a friend, "I might do something for other people's [children] in Leland's name."

Immediately after their return to America, the Stanfords set

Young Leland Stanford Jr. traveled widely with his parents. In June 1883, when he was 15, he and his family left on an extended trip to Europe. On February 11, 1884, he wrote from Naples, Italy, to a friend, Miss Lizzie Hull, about his touring experiences. A month later, he died suddenly in Florence of typhoid fever.

Stanford and his wife spent six months on the East Coast after their son's death, interviewing college presidents and planning the university they would build as a memorial to their child.

their plan in motion by seeking advice from four of the most distinguished and progressive university presidents in America—Charles Eliot, president of Harvard; General Francis A. Walker, president of the Massachusetts Institute of Technology (MIT); Daniel Coit Gilman, president of Johns Hopkins; and Andrew White, president of Cornell. Although the Stanfords had initially considered various memorials to their son—including a museum, a technical institute, and a hospital—Harvard's Eliot recommended that they establish a tuition-free university in California. The Stanfords determined to do so, inspired by the new movement that was liberalizing American higher education. In 1868, Cornell's Andrew White had pioneered this movement, which sought to breathe life into the rigid American curriculum by emphasizing practical and technical education. Eliot had taken the changes further at Harvard by eliminating prescribed courses altogether. In formulating their plans, the Stanfords were impressed by the reforms of both these men, as well as by the academic innovations of Walker, who had reinvented MIT as a center of technology, and by Coit's groundbreaking emphasis at Johns Hopkins on postgraduate research.

On November 14, 1885—a year and eight months after their son's death and eight months after Leland Stanford began his first term as a U.S. senator—the couple formalized their plans to found a university. In a simple ceremony held in the library of their San Francisco mansion, Leland and Jane Stanford presented a Grant of Endowment to the 24 friends and business associates who had agreed to serve as the new university's trustees. According to the founding grant, the Stanfords would leave the great part of their estate—estimated to be between $20 million and $30 million—to the new Leland Stanford Junior University established in memory of their son. The gift, unprecedented in size, attracted widespread comment in the press. Editors of *The New York Times* predicted that "the enormous sum given by its founder should, if wisely expended, create a university whose fame will not be confined to America." London's *Daily Telegraph*, too, marveled at the huge grant, declaring it would make Stanford University's endowment the largest "in the history of mankind."

The site where the Stanfords planned to build their University was the much beloved center of their family life—the Palo Alto Farm, a bucolic estate of plains and rolling hills. In 1876 they had purchased 650 acres so that their son could have the benefits of an outdoor life, and their holdings had gradually expanded to 8,800 acres. Leland Stanford had named the farm after El Palo Alto (Spanish for "high stick"), the nearly 1,000-year-old redwood that towered more than 100 feet over the north corner of the property—a landmark that had been well known to Spanish explorers a century before. The estate was lushly planted with vineyards, orchards, vegetables, and grain. It was most renowned, however, for its elaborate and meticulously kept trotting tracks and stables, as well as the championship horses that Leland Stanford raised according to his own pioneering theories—breeding British thoroughbreds with Kentucky racehorses to produce outstanding steeds. MIT's Walker had visited the farm at the Stanfords' invitation. Following his advice, the founders hired the distinguished landscape architect Frederick Law Olmsted—designer of New York's Central Park—and the architectural firm of Shepley, Rutan, and Coolidge to design and construct the Stanford campus.

The Stanfords named their Palo Alto Farm after a twin-trunked redwood tree, known as El Palo Alto (below). When the University first opened, surveyor's stakes—labeled with literary street names such as Kipling, Webster, and Melville—marked the outlines of the new town of University Park, which was soon renamed Palo Alto and incorporated in 1894.

The Palo Alto Stock Farm

IN 1876 THE STANFORDS began acquiring land in the Santa Clara Valley, south of San Francisco. To improve his health, Governor Stanford took up horse trotting as a pastime and quickly became engrossed in the breeding and development of horses. His vast Palo Alto Stock Farm was the world's largest breeding farm for trotters, renowned for the celebrated sire Electioneer and championship steeds including Arion, Sunol, and Palo Alto.

The Palo Alto Stock Farm was also the place where the world's first motion picture was produced. Stanford had hired a photographer named Eadweard Muybridge to photograph his horses in motion. To accomplish this, Muybridge used numerous cameras rigged with electrically controlled shutters. The result of their collaboration was a landmark photographic study, *The Horse in Motion*, and the first moving picture—created when Muybridge projected the images, in sequence, onto a screen at the Stanfords' Palo Alto home.

Leland Stanford Jr. on his pony Palo. Alto. May 1879

photographed. may 1879 by Eadweard Muybridge

A series of 8 phases of a stride by a pony while cantering. photographed on wet collodion plate. E.M.

17 18 19 20 21 22 23 24 25 26

24-1

On May 14, 1887—the 19th anniversary of the birth of Leland Stanford, Jr.—the University's cornerstone was laid. By then, the master plan—created by Olmsted in close collaboration with architect Charles A. Coolidge and the senator himself—was already substantially in place. The University would be organized around a central courtyard or "inner quad," framed by a continuous quadrangle of arcades and single-story buildings. Echoing in design the Franciscan missions of California, the buildings and arcades, with their striking red-tile roofs and Moorish and baroque influences, would be constructed of buff-colored sandstone quarried at New Almaden near the town of San Jose. Jane Stanford, a tall, strong, straightforward woman with "a commanding presence"—and a capable carpenter herself—took great interest in the building project. Mrs. Stanford personally supervised much of the construction work, using the tip of her parasol to measure the depth of stone carving and ordering architectural details removed and added to her liking.

While the physical structure of the University was taking shape, Leland and Jane Stanford turned to the task of recruiting a president and faculty. Although Stanford initially offered the presidency to Walker, the MIT president had declined to make the move to California. Cornell's Andrew White also refused the position, but he urged the senator to approach White's former student, David Starr Jordan, a 40-year-old natural science professor who had served six years as president of Indiana University at Bloomington. The Stanfords set out for Bloomington that very evening, and immediately after interviewing Jordan, Stanford offered him the presidency. Just as

Above: *The Stanfords commissioned Frederick Law Olmsted to create the landscape and overall master plan of their university. Olmsted, who had designed New York's Central Park, originally proposed a less formal, more naturalistic arrangement than the monumental plan the Stanfords ultimately chose.* Left: *Stone cutters chisel the Quad's sandstone, quarried near San Jose.*

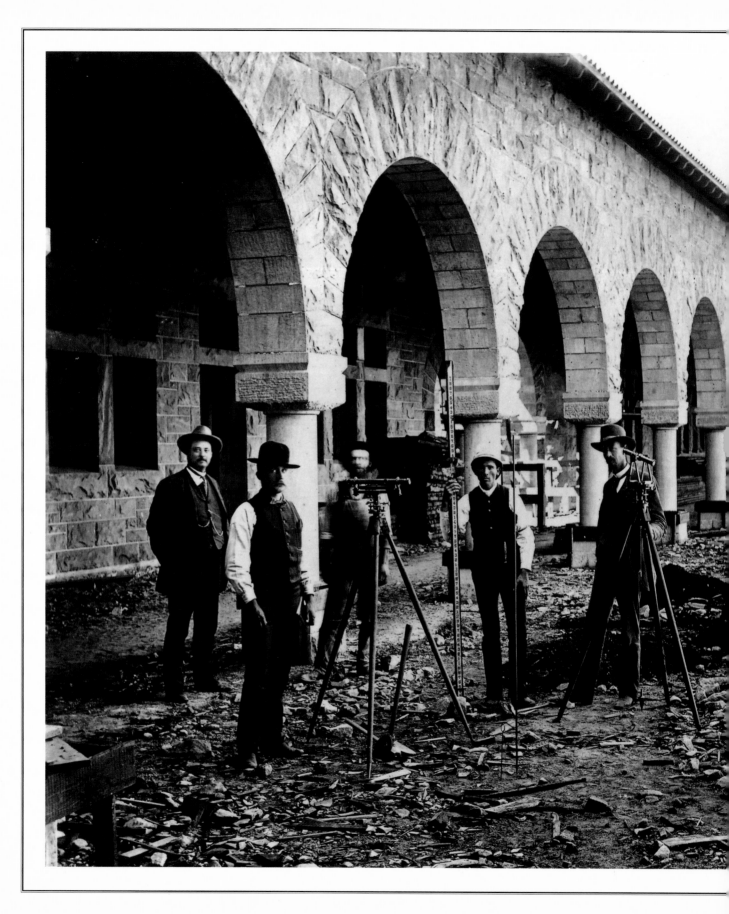

Building the University

BY THE TIME STANFORD University opened in 1891, 12 buildings of the Inner Quad plus Encina Hall, the men's dormitory, and Roble Hall, the women's residence, were completed. On dusty Alvarado Row, ten faculty cottages had been erected, but professors' families still had to draw their drinking water in buckets from a well.

President Jordan took on the task of naming all the campus streets for important figures in California history and dubbed the irrigation reservoir on campus "Lagunita."

In 1900, during the University's next great building boom—known as the "second Stone Age"—the main entrance of the Outer Quad was marked by the 10-story-high Memorial Arch. Work continued for more than two years longer on the Arch's ornamentation, which featured a frieze entitled "The Progress of Civilization in America." The arch collapsed during the 1906 earthquake and was never reconstructed. *Left:* Surveyors at work in the Inner Quad.

U NTIL IT TUMBLED IN THE 1906 earthquake, a 100-foot-tall smokestack—said to be the most symmetrical ever constructed—towered over the campus power plant. Beneath the smokestack is a view of newly constructed faculty housing on (from right to left) Lasuen, Salvatierra, and Alvarado Row. *Below:* Trowel used to lay Stanford's cornerstone on May 14, 1887.

A Lavish Remembrance

I N 1899, SIX YEARS AFTER Leland Stanford died, construction began on the original Memorial Church. Jane Stanford dedicated it to her husband in 1903.

The Romanesque design, inspired in part by Trinity Church in Boston, was adorned with rich fittings and ornaments. In Venice, Mrs. Stanford commissioned mosaics—many of them depicting stories from the Old Testament—to cover the interior walls and outer façade of the church. In Florence, she commissioned marble statues of the Apostles for the chancel. Nineteen stained glass windows illustrated scenes from the life of Christ, and a copy of Rosselli's *Last Supper* was placed behind the altar. The church was destroyed by the great earthquake of 1906 and rebuilt—without its tower—at a cost of $1.2 million.

quickly, Jordan accepted. "I might have found a more famous educator," Stanford explained to a reporter, "but I desired a comparatively young man who would grow up with the University." The educational ideas of the two men coincided closely, Jordan recalled, and "the possibilities were so challenging to one of my temperament that I could not decline."

The new president set to work immediately recruiting Stanford's first faculty—mostly young, adventurous professors from Cornell, Johns Hopkins, and the University of Indiana—and designing an innovative academic program. At Stanford, as at Harvard and Cornell, students would have freedom of choice, but the new Stanford system would not permit them to "flit from one subject to another, acquiring versatility without real training." The Stanford plan, under Jordan, would encourage mastery as well as freedom. Each student would select a "major professor" for an advisor in his or her first year and then set about fulfilling the courses required by that professor. Beyond those studies, students were free to take elective courses. There would be no grades; students would receive a simple plus or minus, reflecting Jordan's belief that "marks and terms are clumsy devices, more suitable for measuring cordwood than culture."

Jordan and the Stanfords were in complete agreement that women and men should be enrolled at Stanford University on equal terms. In his first address to the University's trustees in 1885, Leland Stanford had declared that he and his wife deemed it "of the first importance that the education of both sexes shall be equally full and complete, varied only as nature dictates. The *rights* of one sex, political and otherwise, are the same as those of the other sex, and this equality of rights ought to be fully recognized." When the University opened, the students who registered for the fall semester included 130 women, 255 freshmen, 116 upperclassmen who had transferred to

David Starr Jordan, Stanford's first president, was a respected ichthyologist and had served as president of Indiana University at Bloomington from 1885 to 1891. A member of Cornell University's first graduating class, he was influenced by the liberal educational ideas of Cornell president Andrew D. White. It was White who urged the Stanfords to recruit Jordan, "one of the leading scientific men of the country, possessed of a most charming power of literary expression, with a remarkable ability in organization, and blessed with good sound sense."

Stanford from 25 different colleges across the country, and 37 graduate students. Also enrolled were 147 "special" students—mostly working-class men, ages 20 and older, who were eager for the opportunity to study. The initial enrollment of 555 immediately established Stanford as California's largest academic institution.

Clearly, 15 faculty members would not be sufficient to teach such a populous student body. Senator Stanford had originally insisted on that small number of professors, expecting that no more than 250 students would register. Jordan, however, had responded quickly to the larger-than-expected enrollment and made advance arrangements so that, shortly after opening day, 30 faculty members were listed on the roster. Among them were geologist John Casper Branner, Jordan's undergraduate classmate at Cornell, and a lone female faculty member, Mary Sheldon Barnes, who was recruited as assistant professor of history. In addition to the resident faculty members, Jordan and the senator persuaded a number of highly prominent individuals—including former U.S. president Benjamin Harrison and Cornell president Andrew White—to teach at Stanford as nonresident lecturers.

Undergraduates pore over copies of the University's year-book, the Stanford Quad, *which was first published by the Class of 1895.*

JUNIOR QUAD APPEARS.

For nearly everyone that first year, the sense of freedom and adventure far outweighed the considerable physical discomforts. For students, according to one graduate, Stanford offered "something in the pioneer tradition, …an emphasis on individual effort and the individual's right to succeed on his own terms, …academic leeway…, and an energy which sprang from the circumstances of its birth." At Stanford, there was a general expectation "that you would stretch yourself in whatever you undertook." Like academics,

campus life was relatively free and unrestrained. "We have no rules here," Jordan announced to the freshman class. "We merely expect you to act like ladies and gentlemen. But, if you do not," he threatened, "we will pick you up by the nape of the neck, carry you to the edge of campus, and drop you off." Professors—who averaged around 30 years of age—mixed freely with their pupils, forming close, informal friendships. Together they made the best of taxing situations. Until class bells began operating, periods were marked, Western-style, by the clanging of a triangle hung inside an archway. In wet weather, the dirt streets and roads turned into rivers of thick mud. Microscopes, books, faculty, and—most problematically—housing were in chronic short supply. Bachelor professors lodged with male students in Encina Hall, demonstrating good-natured patience when students amused themselves by dropping water-filled bags out windows and smashing up the furniture. Women students were domiciled in Roble Hall, with

Biology students learn dissection techniques.

In Stanford's early years, each class wore its own distinctive hats—freshman beanies, sophomore porkpies, junior plug hats (above), and senior sombreros (top right). There was annual mayhem during the frosh-soph mudfight and the Plug Ugly, when seniors tried to smash the juniors' plugs.

its pink-and-blue parlor and soft, white, blue-bordered blankets on the beds (the red blankets of Encina were woven from the wool of Stanford sheep). Fewer than half the students, however, could be accommodated by the two dormitories. Many young men who were unable to find housing in faculty homes or the nearby villages of Mayfield or Menlo Park settled in at "the Camp," a cluster of whitewashed shacks originally built to house construction workers. This shantylike but spirited establishment provided cheap quarters for male students "who were not the fraternity kind" or could not afford Encina. The Camp also served up palatable meals that were widely preferred to the dorms' standard fare of beans, mutton, and prunes—supplemented by black walnuts and fat grapes freely pilfered (by students and faculty alike) from the Stanford vineyards.

Jordan, a great and shaggy presence, set the tone for the friendly, informal atmosphere on campus. Widely admired by both students and professors, he would often stop by unannounced at dormitories and fraternity houses to chat casually with students over lunch or dinner. He also relished competing in the annual faculty and senior baseball games, in which bizarrely attired students ran bases dressed in ballet costumes and Mother Hubbards.

A sense of bold, irreverent fun seemed to inspire many of Stanford's new "traditions," including the distinctive headgear worn by lower and upperclassmen. Freshmen wore beanies, sophomores donned porkpie hats, seniors sported field hats or "sombreros," and juniors were known for their hideously adorned "plugs"— lead-painted, misshapen top hats that later featured prominently in the "Plug Ugly," a weird, strictly Stanford ceremony. During the event, which debuted in October 1898, an eight-foot-tall plug hat was carried out in a mock procession, after which seniors promptly set upon the juniors in an attempt to smash their plugs. By 1913, the Plug Ugly had degenerated into a violent battle between seniors and juniors, and the event was banned.

Students were quick to attend to more serious matters as well, organizing the Associated Students of Stanford University (ASSU); the first campus publication—the monthly *Palo Alto*; and organizations ranging from the Law Debating Society to the ladies' glee club, all during the University's first year. The first small graduating class— made up of seniors who had transferred to the University from other schools—formed the Stanford Alumni Association on Commencement Day in June 1892. Five fraternities, too, beginning with Zeta Psi, and one sorority—Kappa Alpha Theta—quickly established chapters on campus.

And of course, from the beginning, there was football. Although campus athletes—male and female—took part in sports including basketball, track and field, swimming, and tennis, it was football that captured center stage in student life. The first game against Berkeley took place on March 19, 1892, when Stanford's novice football team, managed by a freshman named Herbert Hoover (later 31st president of the United States) faced the Cal squad on a sandlot at San Francisco's Haight and Stanyan Streets. As a crowd of

Editors of the **Stanford Daily,** **Chaparral** *and* **Sequoia** *peruse each others' publications. The* **Sequoia,** *launched in December 1891, was the University's first student newspaper. The* **Daily** *followed in September 1892, and the humor magazine, the* **Chaparral,** *appeared for the first time in 1899.*

Sports at Center Stage

FROM THE VERY START, athletics played a central part in campus life. President Jordan enjoyed taking part in informal faculty-student baseball games, and organized sports were popular with both men and women.

The Stanford women's basketball team (pictured below, c. 1896) lost its first interscholastic game against Castilleja School in 1894. Two years later, the team won its first intercollegiate game against the University of California, with a score of 2 to 1. The game was played at the Armory in San Francisco; for modesty's sake, no men were permitted in the stands.

Stanford's football team (bottom left) was organized in the University's first year and unexpectedly beat Berkeley in the first Big Game, held in March 1892. Football was banned at Stanford in 1906 and replaced with rugby for 12 years—but American football, and the traditional Big Game, returned in the 1919 season.

Upper Left: Stanford's track team in 1905.

When Stanford opened in 1891, freshman Herbert Hoover was the first student to whom President Jordan assigned a room at Encina Hall. He went on to graduate in 1895 with a BA in geology. After a successful engineering career, Hoover headed war relief operations during and after World War I, served as secretary of commerce in the Harding and Coolidge administrations, and was elected president of the United States in 1928.

nearly 20,000 spectators packed the stands, the Stanford "kidlets" unexpectedly beat the seasoned Berkeley players, 14-10, claiming victory in the very first Big Game. Stanford's first baseball team echoed that triumph the next month, when it pounded Berkeley, 13-6—a win Stanford students celebrated by staging a raucous nightgown parade and painting the Palo Alto railroad station red.

Throughout the first years, Jane Stanford was a familiar figure on the campus—kindhearted, respected, serious, and striking in her silks, bonnets, and brocades. Senator Stanford, however, was frequently away in Washington and appeared increasingly feeble in his few appearances on campus. "He seemed to us an aging man, feeling his age, ready to be rid of burdens and care.... We were sorry for him and loved him," Ellen Coit Elliot remembered. On June 21, 1893, shortly after the University's second commencement, the 69-year-old senator died in his sleep. Upon his death, Jane Stanford, then 65, assumed all responsibilities for the University. It was a nearly devastating burden, since a financial depression and extensive litigation over her husband's estate, brought by the U.S. government, dried up almost all her income. During the more than five "pretty long years" that it took to settle the estate, there was barely enough cash to keep the University going. Jane Stanford designated the University as her main "household" and the faculty as her "servants" in order to fund Stanford through her monthly allowance of $10,000 from the estate—retaining only $350 a month for her personal expenses. The faculty bore their part of the financial burden as well, accepting a 12 percent cut in pay. During those hard times, the University "limped along, short of everything," wrote Edith Mirrielees, later a professor of English. "Chalk came to be doled out by the stick. Pages left blank in examination books served for interdepartment letters. Classrooms went unswept." At last, however, the Supreme Court decided the case in the Stanfords' favor on March 2,

Jane Stanford: Keeping the Doors Open

STRONG, SERIOUS, AND determined, Jane Stanford shared equally with her husband the dream of building Stanford University. After his death in 1893, she assumed full financial responsibility for the University—a difficult and courageous task, given the lengthy litigation that tied up the Stanford estate. During that time, Jane Stanford funded the University out of her own household allowance, retaining a minimal amount for her own expenses. After the estate was released from probate, she devoted herself to completing the University's construction, although the new buildings she commissioned deviated from the Spanish-style architecture of the original plan.

Until her death in 1905, Mrs. Stanford resided at the family home on the Stanford campus (*below*). The house was destroyed during the 1906 earthquake, except for its west wing. In 1920, the surviving wing was leased by the Stanford Home for Convalescent Children. The structure was finally razed in 1966.

1896—a decision celebrated with joyful pandemonium on campus—and the estate was finally released from probate in 1898.

When the financial clouds finally cleared, Jordan's immediate priority was to increase funds for equipment and raise faculty salaries. Jane Stanford, however, chose to focus the University's resources on campus construction. "Feeling that her life might be cut short at any moment," he wrote, "she was feverishly eager to complete, while she could, as much as possible of the original architectural scheme." Under Mrs. Stanford's direction, the Outer Quad buildings, Memorial Arch, and Memorial Church were built, as well as four buildings bordering Palm Drive—a chemistry building, additions to the museum, a new library, and a gymnasium for men. The design of the latter two structures departed radically from the architecture of the original Stanford plan.

Jane Stanford made other major decisions in the years following her husband's death. In 1900, she stirred controversy when she demanded the resignation of Edward A. Ross from the University faculty. Professor Ross had angered her by publicly endorsing political positions and racial biases that she opposed. In protest over Ross's forced resignation, six additional faculty members left the University, including Professor George E. Howard, who was regarded as one of the best teachers at Stanford. It was an episode that divided the campus, raised serious issues of academic freedom, and broke "something of the magic spell" of Stanford's early years.

Another move by Mrs. Stanford had long-lasting consequences for student enrollment. Alarmed that the proportion of women students had risen to nearly 45 percent by 1899—reflecting the higher high school graduation rates of women nationwide—she legally amended the Founding Grant to cap the proportion of women by limiting their enrollment to 500. The rationale, she explained, was that the University was a memorial to a boy and must not appear to be primarily a school for girls. The limit on women was not lifted by Stanford's trustees until 1933, and it was another 40 years before it was legally rescinded.

Above: *From 1892 to 1920, Dr. Clelia Duel Mosher, professor of personal hygiene at Stanford, broke new ground with her study of Victorian women's sexuality. Dr. Mosher—who received her BA and MA from Stanford and graduated from Johns Hopkins Medical School in 1900—surveyed 45 women about their health, personal histories, and sexual practices. Her research represents perhaps the earliest sexual study on women and the first conducted by a female researcher.*

Left: *In 1901, Jane Stanford ordered the construction of several new buildings, including a neoclassical-style library (pictured here) and a new gymnasium for men. Neither structure survived the 1906 quake.*

At the age of 75, Jane Stanford transferred her University powers to the Board of Trustees. Two years later, she died suddenly during a midwinter visit to Honolulu. Following her death, the trustees announced that all campus construction would be completed by spring 1906, and that more funds would be made available for salaries and academic programs. Stanford University, at last, seemed poised to realize the academic promise that Jordan and the founders had long envisioned. In March 1906, William James, America's preeminent philosopher and psychologist, pointed to the University's bright future in a Founders' Day address he delivered while on leave from Harvard as a visiting Stanford professor: "Let [Stanford] not imitate; let her lead, not follow.… Not vast but intense; less a place for teaching youths and maidens than for training scholars; devoted to truth, radiating influence, setting standards." Compared to the "purity and serenity" of the tranquil Stanford campus, James declared, "Eastern institutions look all dark and huddled and confused."

Only weeks later, however, disaster shook the Stanford campus. At 5:13 on the morning of April 18, 1906, a massive earthquake struck the San Francisco Bay Area, estimated at 8.25 on the Richter scale. In approximately 70 seconds of destruction, much of the newly completed University was reduced to rock and rubble. In the Quadrangle, gray dust swirled around the wreckage of Memorial Church, with its tumbled mosaics and collapsed spire. The new Memorial Arch was a crumbled wreck. The just-completed library and

Left: The earthquake hurled a statue of zoologist Louis Agassiz headfirst into the pavement—leading one Stanford wit to remark that "Agassiz was great in the abstract but not in the concrete." The marble statue suffered only a broken nose and was soon restored to its perch outside the second floor of the Zoology Department. **Below:** *Memorial Church in ruins.*

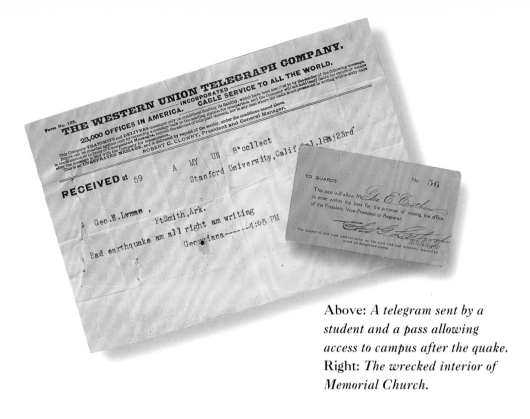

Above: *A telegram sent by a student and a pass allowing access to campus after the quake.* Right: *The wrecked interior of Memorial Church.*

gymnasium had turned into mere piles of masonry, and a marble statue of Harvard zoologist Louis Agassiz had plunged from the second story of the Zoology Department, imbedding itself upside down in the concrete. The University's immense powerhouse smokestack fell, killing a night fireman, Otto Gerdes. A second man, a student named Junius Hanna, was killed when the Encina chimney crashed through to the basement. Although Roble's third floor collapsed into the first-floor parlor, no students in that dorm were seriously injured.

Fearful of structural damage and aftershocks, everyone camped outdoors for days. Refugees from Encina found temporary homes in nearby shrubbery, nicknamed "Easy Street," and a fraternity set up housekeeping on a tennis court. Relief teams from Stanford were dispatched to San Francisco, remaining in the burning city after other relief forces had departed. There was no hurry to return to campus. Jordan had announced that all classes would be canceled for the remainder of the school year, although degrees would be awarded to candidates who were in good standing.

Physically, the University was crippled by the quake. By fall quarter, the only buildings that had been sufficiently repaired were, for

No. 26.   ENCINA HALL STANFORD UNIVERSITY
APR 18 '06.

We're "Up Against It."

For a few days after the quake, everyone set up house-keeping outdoors. Students made camp in the shrubs outside Encina, and fraternity men put up lace curtains in their temporary quarters on the tennis court.
Right: *Bristol's Recording Volt Meter, a predecessor of the Richter scale, calibrated the power of the 1906 quake.*

the most part, the well-constructed Inner and Outer Quadrangles, Encina Hall, and Roble. The cost to replace the damaged buildings was calculated to be more than $3 million, and nearly half that amount—$1.2 million—would be needed to rebuild Memorial Church. Many of Jordan's grand plans and hopes also came crashing down in the temblor's wake. "During the past seven years we have been spending our income to build, …and we were nearly done," he told students soon after the earthquake. "We were looking forward toward greater intensification, toward improvements and the largest, best, and most expensive faculty of any university; but we will now have to begin again, to return to our stone age." The new library, gym, Memorial Arch, and museum annex, the University decided, would not be rebuilt. No major new campus construction projects would be undertaken for a decade. Instead, Stanford's near-term future would be marked by the grim necessities of reconstruction and retrenchment. "It was now obvious," Jordan wrote, "that the rest of my administration must needs be devoted simply to solidifying what had already been attained."

Gradually, however, as the University recovered from the quake, the president found himself turning his attention from campus affairs to the wider sphere of global politics. In 1910, he was elected chief director of the World Peace Foundation, and in 1913, he retired from the presidency, assuming the newly created role of chancellor. His long-time friend, John Casper Branner—a gifted teacher who had served as chairman of Stanford's Geology Department as well as University vice-president—succeeded Jordan as president. Branner, however, was 63 years old and chose to serve only two years before he, too, retired. In January 1916, Ray Lyman Wilbur, dean of medicine at Stanford and a member of the class of 1896, took office as Stanford University's third president. It was true, as Jordan had once said, that "Rome was not built in a day, nor Stanford in a century; but it is being built, quietly, honestly, steadfastly, stone after stone…." It would be Wilbur's task to equip the University to meet the challenge of the coming age.

Above: *In 1913, geology professor John Casper Branner succeeded David Starr Jordan as Stanford's second president. Branner and Jordan had been close friends and classmates at Cornell and taught together at Indiana University. In 1891, Branner was the first professor invited to join the Stanford faculty. He served as president of Stanford until 1915, when he retired at the age of 65.* **Left:** *Theodore Roosevelt visited the Stanford campus in 1911.*

STEADYING THE COURSE

STANFORD'S EARLY YEARS HAD BEEN MARKED BY rapid growth and rocked by grave misfortune. Now, after a quarter century, it was the task of the University's third president to steer Stanford toward some stability and to secure its standing in higher education. Few doubted that the best man for the job was the formidable Ray Lyman Wilbur, and he was the unanimous choice of the University's trustees. Tall, striking, even Lincoln-like in his appearance, the 40-year-old Wilbur was able and aloof, "a granitic character," as one student described him. What the former University physician lacked at first in popularity he more than made up for by the intensity of his leadership and focus. "All of you won't like him.... But you'll see action under him," the student editor of the *Stanford Illustrated Review* predicted.

Not unexpectedly, Wilbur's first year in office became known as the "year of changes." The new president called into question the entire fabric of the University, from academic programs to social and administrative matters. Above all, Wilbur was determined to raise the caliber of campus scholarship. "The situation at Stanford," he concluded in his memoirs, "was such that young people could be very content to do a minimum amount of work and a maximum of play. Stanford's inviting climate for outdoor activities," he mused, "may have had something to do with it ..., but there was a general trend over the whole country to overemphasize the social aspects, the side shows, of college life." Still, Wilbur was certainly no killjoy. As a Stanford graduate and former professor, the new president knew and appreciated the liberating charms of "the Farm," as the University had

Preceding pages:
Commencement exercises in the Quad in 1915.
Left: *Medical school dean Ray Lyman Wilbur* (left) *waits with Chancellor David Starr Jordan before Wilbur's inauguration as Stanford's third president in 1916.*

Above: *For many years, small flocks of sheep served as Stanford's "automatic lawn mowers and weed eradicators."* **Right:** *Bamboo cane and a sophomore porkpie hat.*

come to be known. "The freedom, the wholesome, unconventional ways, the personal association with enthusiastic teachers, the absence of traditions…all conspired to foster in me a deep love for Stanford," he told students and faculty members in his inaugural address.

But in 1916, the world around Stanford was changing, and challenging times called for a new standard of engagement and scholarly performance. Two years before, World War I had broken out in Europe—and while America was not yet officially at war, the coming emergency "was already in plain sight," Edith Mirrielees recalled. Wilbur believed that the University had become too insular in response to the turmoil of its early years. His goal, he declared, was to broaden Stanford's role and make "the University the recruiting ground for youth, arming them for the big tasks of the race." He moved quickly and decisively to put Stanford on an expansive academic track—strengthening graduate study, increasing academic rigor, promoting faculty research and consulting, and replacing semesters with the quarter system to make full use of the University year round. Although letter grades had been instituted in 1911, Wilbur introduced a grade-point system for evaluating students. "Quality and not quantity is the Stanford ideal," he declared in a letter to the faculty. "Certainly it is at least as important to know what the score is in the academic or scholastic field as it is in athletics."

Wilbur took an especially hard line with Stanford fraternities— whose members consistently ranked in the bottom third of students—by ordering them to boost their academic performance within two years or risk severe disciplinary action. In his efforts to raise scholarship and curb undergraduate distractions, Wilbur even took his case directly to parents and students. In a stern August 1916 letter, he informed them that: "A student's principal business is his studies.... It takes time to run an automobile, and it often leads to life off the campus, to extravagance and much foolish-  ness.... The student who cannot be content to lead the simple, clean, industrious life expected on the Stanford campus should go elsewhere."

The new president's reforms were not always appreciated— especially by alumni who, in their student days, had relished a more carefree university environment. One critic of the president's occasionally brusque style commented that "Dr. Wilbur had spent too many years telling people to stick out their tongues." Nevertheless, he was making a clear impact on Stanford. "Even a very young student in a very young university could sense that he was in the presence of something extraordinary," recalled one undergraduate from Wilbur's early years. "It was not just the unique environment of elbow room. Underneath was the spirit of a 'university of high degree,' a demand for excellence. And after a while, we discovered, still deeper, the steel core of this structure: the personality and character of Dr. Ray Lyman Wilbur."

Above: *In 1917, the French government awarded this Croix de Guerre to the First Stanford Unit of the American Ambulance Field Service in France, in appreciation of its outstanding wartime service.*
Right: *During World War I, student soldiers drilled under the tutelage of Major Bugge, professor of military training and tactics, and the army used Encina and Sequoia halls as barracks.*

In the years before the war, Europe and its mounting political tensions had seemed very "far away from the tawny hills of the Santa Clara Valley," Bruce Bliven, a 1911 graduate, remembered. Closer to home, and more compelling, was the allure of silent movies; the new "progressive dancing"; 3-course, 25-cent meals at "the Greek's" in Palo Alto; and languid afternoons at Searsville Lake. The Stanford campus had taken little note of events such as Peary's discovery of the North Pole, the revolution in Mexico, and the creation of the Chinese Republic—world affairs, Bliven recalled, that "were hardly more than the hum of angry bees far off across a drowsy landscape." But in April 1917, the hum grew louder as America went to war, and Stanford men and women lined up behind the effort. The year before, Wilbur had instituted military training on the campus, and two members of the Stanford community—assistant professor of Romance languages Robert Edouard Pellissier and James Grant Fergusson, '08—had been killed in battle in France. Now, masses of students—including nearly all male sophomores, juniors, and seniors—left Stanford to enlist in "the war to end all wars." In 1917, the First Stanford Ambulance Unit departed for France. Numbers of students attended the University commencement dressed in uniform, and the army commandeered Encina Hall as a barracks. Stanford alumnae went to the front as volunteers with the Red Cross and worked in the fields harvesting crops in the Santa Clara Valley. With so many of the men gone off to war, women stepped into leadership positions on campus. For the first time, women students served as managing editor and news editor of the *Daily* and made up the majority of the newspaper's reporters.

Stanford was stung by a degree of criticism during the war years because of David Starr Jordan's high-profile work in support of pacifism. There was even some suspicion of the University because of its unofficial German motto *Die Luft der Freiheit Weht* ("The Wind of Freedom Blows")—a phrase originated by Ulrich von Hutten, a 16th-century German humanist who had argued for secular freedom. But

Stanford's reputation also benefited during and after World War I from the extraordinary efforts and foresight of its most prominent alumnus and trustee, Herbert Clark Hoover, '95. As early as 1914, Hoover and his wife, Lou Henry Hoover, '98, had launched a privately funded relief campaign to avert famine in Belgium—a country overrun by German troops and almost completely dependent on imports for its food. The Hoovers had recruited many Stanford people to staff the humanitarian effort, which expanded as the war progressed, importing and distributing tens of thousands of tons of rations each month to residents of Belgium and northern France.

As an eyewitness to the unfolding of World War I in Europe, Hoover was inspired by the memoirs of Cornell president Andrew White, who had collected an immense number of documents and

World War I relief workers, directed by Herbert Hoover, shipped millions of pounds of flour to Belgium in flour sacks like the one below, from the Hoover Institution Archives. After the war, the Belgians elaborately decorated the empty sacks, returning many of them to the United States as tokens of thanks.

"fugitive publications" on the French Revolution while living in France as a student in the 1850s. As early as 1915, Hoover resolved to begin his own collection of contemporary wartime documents. In 1919, while heading the American Relief Administration and channeling food throughout Europe after the Armistice, he enlisted Stanford historians in collecting pamphlets, propaganda, government documents, foreign newspapers, and other wartime literature, an effort he personally funded. A team of Stanford collectors fanned out across Europe to assemble the Hoover War History Collection, sending vast quantities of materials back to the University on returning ships that had carried food to Europe. Wilbur admiringly referred to Hoover as "the greatest packrat of all time because, whenever he leaves a ton of food, he picks up a pound of history." Accordingly, the huge collecting project became known as "Operation Packrat."

Wilbur, along with students and faculty, stepped beyond his University role during the war. In 1917, when President Wilson named Herbert Hoover as the head of the U.S. Food Administration, Hoover in turn recruited Wilbur to serve as his chief deputy. After the Armistice, Wilbur returned to his Stanford duties and once again faced the challenge of building up the University's standards and resources. This time, the most pressing problems were financial. Costs of equipment and materials had climbed rapidly after the war, and additional housing was urgently needed for the expanding student body and faculty. In addition, new facilities were needed for the Medical School—the former Cooper Medical College of San Francisco, which Stanford had acquired in 1908—and academic salaries were alarmingly low. Hoover calculated that Stanford's assistant professors and instructors were taking home less pay than the laborers who were building his spacious new campus home on San Juan Hill. If these problems were not quickly addressed,

Wilbur knew, Stanford could lose its best professors and risk undermining the very quality of its reputation. The University, however, lacked the wherewithal to fund these badly needed improvements, as rising expenditures already outstripped its endowment income.

To help return the University to sound financial footing, students were finally asked to bear part of the cost of their education. Tuition was established for undergraduates for the first time in January 1920, rising from $40 each quarter to $75 each quarter by October 1921. Some Stanford farm property in Gridley and Vina, California, was sold, and the University commenced a large-scale fundraising campaign. Jane Stanford had, during her lifetime, banned public appeals for money, considering them humiliating in the face of the University's apparent wealth. After the costly Medical School was added, however, some outside gifts had been accepted. Now, in 1922, the University turned to alumni and other sources with its first major $3 million drive, the "One Million, Two Million, Three Million" campaign led by Herbert Hoover. The first million dollars was to be earmarked for salaries, the second million would be spent on new construction, and

The worldwide "Spanish flu" epidemic struck the Stanford campus in 1918, straining medical resources and killing six Stanford faculty members and students. Influenza masks were required attire in all classes, and a fraternity house was turned into a makeshift hospital for female students.

the third million would help fund the Medical School. "If the University is to continue to grow," Hoover explained, "it must be by support it shall receive from now on from its own graduates." Although only the first million-dollar goal was fully achieved, the campaign set a precedent for fundraising activities.

"Universities," Wilbur later reflected in 1933, "make their greatest advances when they have *new* money or *no* money. New money," he noted, "makes it possible to accept the many opportunities that are ever open to university men. No money requires the most careful analysis of existing plans and programs and permits a certain amount of pruning, which is a recurring necessity." Throughout the '20s, Wilbur continued this second course of thoughtful "pruning" and academic reform, while steadily raising the scholarly profile of the University. To encourage academic mastery as well as freedom of

Students learn laboratory techniques from botany professor Ira Wiggins.

choice, Wilbur eliminated Jordan's major-professor
system, by which a student's course of study was
determined by a single professor. Although the
intentions of the system had been admirable,
Wilbur explained, "its best feature, the opportunity of
the expert to advise and assist the student in planning his own
education, has been sadly neglected in some departments." To
strengthen the breadth and quality of undergraduate education, a
number of required courses were established for Stanford freshmen
and sophomores for the first time, including foreign language study,
some laboratory science, and a course on American politics, society, and
economics called Problems of Citizenship. At the same time, Wilbur
retained some academic flexibility by introducing independent study
for juniors and seniors.

Wilbur instilled discipline in the University's administrative
structure, too, gradually organizing or "regrouping" the many indepen-

*The Knoll, a 30-room Spanish
Colonial Revival mansion,
was built in 1918 as the home
of president Ray Lyman
Wilbur. Since 1944, Stanford
presidents have lived in the
smaller, less formal Lou
Henry Hoover House, and the
music department has long
occupied the Knoll.*

The Ryan High Voltage Laboratory, named for electrical engineering professor Harris J. Ryan, opened in 1926 with a dramatic display of man-made lightning. Over the years, researchers in the lab solved many problems associated with the long-distance transmission of electric power.

dent departments into schools. The School of Education was formed in 1917, Biological Sciences and Nursing in 1922, Social Sciences in 1923, Engineering in 1925, and both Physical Sciences and Letters in 1925. Stanford was also gradually building its reputation as a center of graduate education and scholarly research. In 1921, Hoover initiated the Stanford Food Research Institute, aided by a grant from the Carnegie Corporation. Also at the urging of Hoover, then secretary of commerce in the Coolidge administration, the Graduate School of

Business opened in 1925 with 16 students under dean Willard E.
Hotchkiss. It was Stanford's fifth professional school, after Medicine,
Education, Nursing, and Law, and only the second business graduate
school in the nation after Harvard's. The following year, Stanford
professor Harris J. Ryan, president of the American Institute of
Engineers, presided over the dramatic campus opening of the Ryan
High Voltage Laboratory, financed by five electric companies and the
City of Los Angeles. The lab—which played a major role in enabling

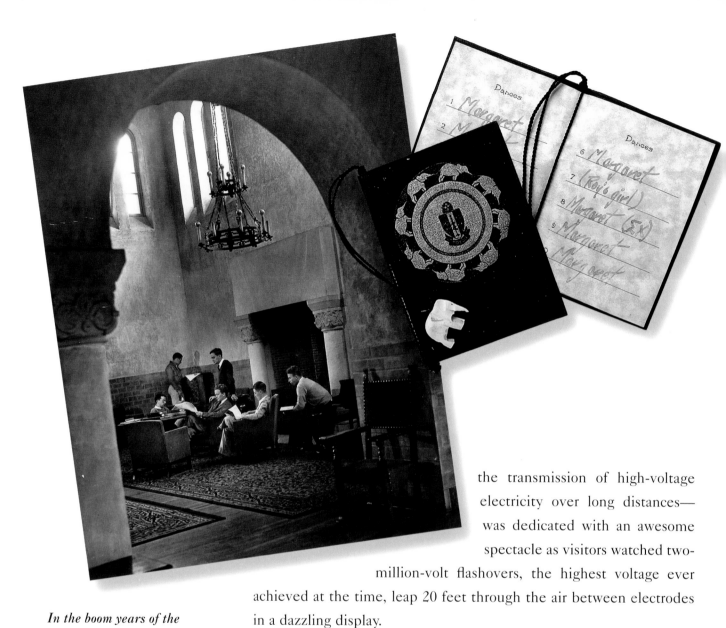

In the boom years of the 1920s, the campus began to develop a sophisticated new "country club" image.
The pioneering, blue-collar "Stanford Roughs" had all but vanished into campus lore.
Above: *Toyon Hall and a dance card from Toyon's 1930 Winter Formal.*
Right: *The courtyard of Roble Gym.*

the transmission of high-voltage electricity over long distances—was dedicated with an awesome spectacle as visitors watched two-million-volt flashovers, the highest voltage ever achieved at the time, leap 20 feet through the air between electrodes in a dazzling display.

Campus life changed in many ways, too, after the war. The working-class "Stanford roughs" of the early days had by and large disappeared by the 1920s. In their place were upper-middle-class students with ample spending money provided by their families' rising stock portfolios. Fewer students now "earned while they learned," and Stanford began to acquire a tony new "country club" image. Defying Prohibition, students drank homemade gin at "Friday fizz frisks," tossed oranges out the windows of Encina Hall at the campus's rustic transportation system known as the "Toonerville Trolley," and rocketed recklessly in their motorcars along Palm Drive—a practice

that contributed to an alarming increase in automobile accidents.

One Encina resident at the time was a Salinas High School graduate named John Steinbeck, who spent many campus evenings reading his stories aloud to any friends who would listen. Shy, sullen, and stubbornly independent, Steinbeck was placed on academic probation and at one time dismissed from the University for poor performance. The trouble, he wrote later, was that "once in college I...got to going to the library and reading what I wanted instead of what was required. I got so far behind that I could not possibly catch up." Nonetheless, in the course of the author's rocky, five-year career at Stanford, his remarkable writing ability earned him the respect of two formidable English professors—the prim and exacting Edith Mirrielees and the fierce Margery Bailey, a "dragon" of a professor who "ate students for breakfast." Steinbeck eventually gave up on college, departing Stanford without a degree in 1925.

John Steinbeck, winner of the 1962 Nobel Prize for Literature, attended Stanford between 1920 and 1925. **Below:** *A first edition of his novel* Cannery Row *and a letter Steinbeck wrote on stationery from Stanford's Fallen Leaf Lodge.*

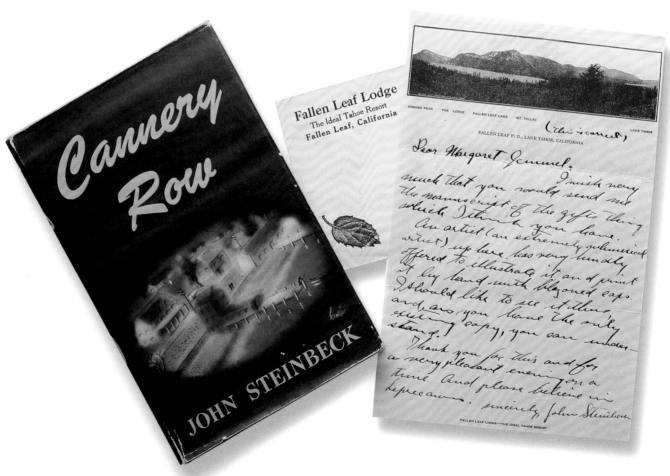

Football, inevitably, returned to the heart of student life after the war. Because of its increasing violence, the sport had been replaced in 1906 by rugby. In 1919, Stanford students voted to bring football back, and in 1921 a new, sixty-thousand-seat Stanford stadium opened just in time for the Big Game. Designed by engineering professors Charles B. Wing, Charles D.

Below: *Ernie Nevers, '26, a football legend under Stanford coach Pop Warner* (left), *was declared the greatest college player of all time by* Sports Illustrated *in 1962. In 1969, he was named to the NCAA's All-Time, All-America team.*

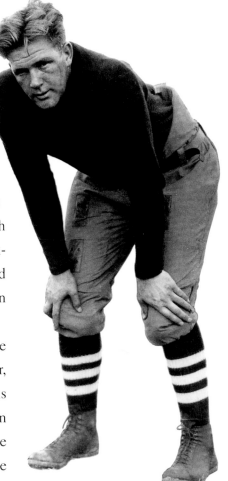

Marx, and William F. Durand, the horseshoe-shaped arena—second only to Yale's in seating capacity—was constructed in four and a half months. The $211,000 project involved one of the nation's last huge earth-moving operations employing horse- and mule-pulled wagons. Glenn "Pop" Warner arrived as Stanford's head coach in 1924, and with star fullback Ernie "Big Dog" Nevers, turned Stanford's football team into a national powerhouse. Nevers, the best fullback in the country and one of the greatest college players of all time, passed, plunged, and punted in the 1925 Rose Bowl game against Notre Dame, playing with two recently fractured ankles bound with bandages, tape, and parts of inner tube. His jersey—bearing the number "1"—was the first ever retired at Stanford. In 1926 the Stanford squad was awarded the Rissman National Trophy as the best team in the nation, the only time the University has ever won that honor.

Other sports were thriving, too. Under diving coach Ernie Brandsten, who arrived in 1916, Stanford divers swept the gold, silver, and bronze medals in the men's springboard and platform competitions at the 1924 Olympic Games. Three Stanford athletes competed in track and field at the 1920 Antwerp Olympic Games and carried home four Olympic medals. And Stanford track continued its powerhouse

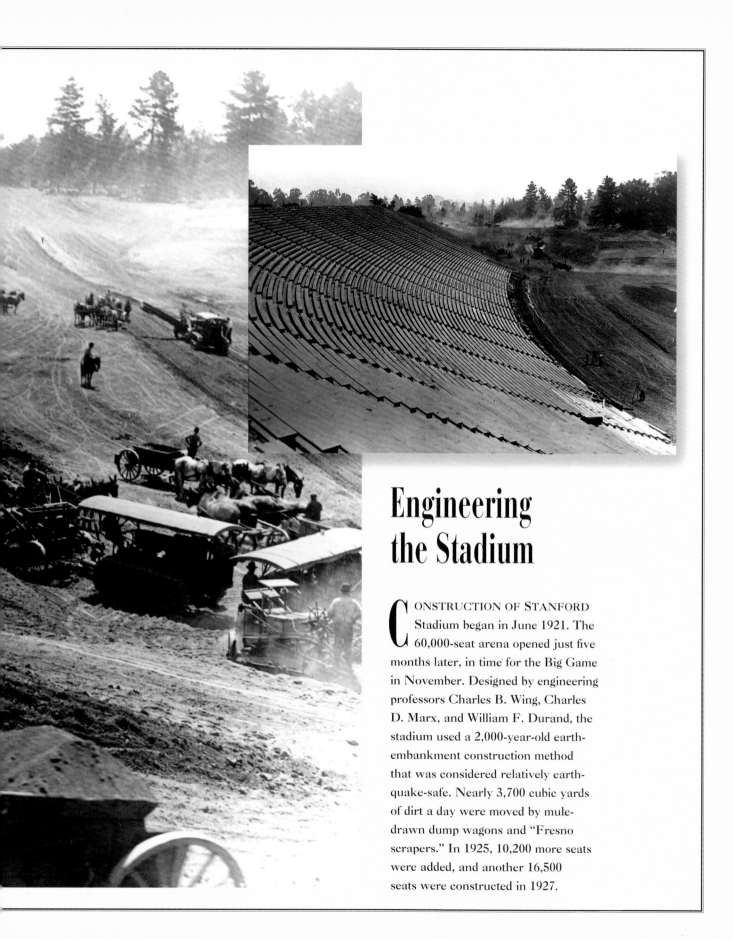

Engineering the Stadium

CONSTRUCTION OF STANFORD Stadium began in June 1921. The 60,000-seat arena opened just five months later, in time for the Big Game in November. Designed by engineering professors Charles B. Wing, Charles D. Marx, and William F. Durand, the stadium used a 2,000-year-old earth-embankment construction method that was considered relatively earth-quake-safe. Nearly 3,700 cubic yards of dirt a day were moved by mule-drawn dump wagons and "Fresno scrapers." In 1925, 10,200 more seats were added, and another 16,500 seats were constructed in 1927.

performance after R. L. "Dink" Templeton arrived as coach in 1921. Over the next 19 seasons, his teams captured 3 NCAA championships, and his Stanford athletes set 16 world records, took 22 national individual titles, and won 2 gold medals in the 1928 Amsterdam Olympics—Bill King in the high jump and Bud Spencer in the 1,600-meter relay.

For Stanford, the decade ended in jubilation. On August 11, 1928, alumnus Herbert Hoover accepted the Republican nomination for president of the United States in a speech broadcast to millions from Stanford Stadium. On Election Day, the candidate cast his ballot on the Stanford campus, and the next day—November 7, 1928—he and his wife received the news of his victory at their campus home. Two thousand Stanford students and other well-wishers—"virtually the whole population of the Farm"—paraded to his house in celebration. The exuberant throng was led by the visiting John Philip Sousa and his seventy-piece band, which trumpeted "The Star Spangled Banner" while a circling airplane fired a twenty-one-shell star-bomb salute. "It was a personal, affectionate tribute to a Stanford man and woman from many Stanford men and women," the *Daily* reported. The elation lasted through Inauguration Day, when classes were canceled so that students could hear the ceremonies over a nationwide radio broadcast.

Hoover brought his trusted friend Ray Lyman Wilbur with him to Washington, D. C., to serve as secretary of the interior, and chemistry professor Robert Eckles Swain took over as acting University president during Wilbur's leave from 1929 to 1933. Hard times, however, quickly followed the euphoria of Hoover's election. On "Black Tuesday"—October 29, 1929—the stock market crashed, and by 1931, nearly five million Americans were unemployed. With the country in the grips of the Depression, Hoover lost his bid for reelection the next year, in a landslide defeat, to Franklin Roosevelt. Again, Hoover and his wife received the election news at their Stanford residence on San Juan Hill—but this time, the president, appearing "tired and sagging," according to a freshman at the scene, delivered only a

Ernie Brandsten (left), *aquatic coach from 1916 to 1947, led Stanford swimmers and divers to 15 Olympic medals. Divers Dave Fall* (middle) *and Pete Desjardins* (right) *each claimed a silver medal in the 1924 Olympic Games. Desjardins went on to capture two golds in the 1928 Olympics.*
Above: *Memorabilia from Herbert Hoover's 1928 presidential campaign.*

Presidential Politics

T HE 1928 PRESIDENTIAL election was memorable for the Stanford University community. Alumnus Herbert Hoover, '95, accepted the Republican nomination for president before a crowd of supporters that packed Stanford Stadium. On election day, he and his wife, Lou Henry Hoover, '98, (below, with their son, Allan) cast their ballots at Stanford. That night, they received news of Hoover's landslide victory at the campus home (right) they had built on San Juan Hill.

The moment climaxed Hoover's long, close ties with the University. Since graduating in Stanford's pioneer class, Hoover had served as a University trustee; established the Hoover Institution on War, Revolution and Peace; and spearheaded creation of the Stanford Food Research Institute and Stanford Graduate School of Business.

Four years later, Hoover ended his unsuccessful 1932 reelection campaign at Stanford and learned of his loss to Franklin Roosevelt at his Stanford home. In 1944, Hoover turned the residence over to the University for use as the official home of Stanford's presidents.

Sam McDonald (right, with President Wilbur), *superintendent of athletic buildings and grounds, was a popular figure on campus from 1903 until his retirement in 1954. Famous for his barbecues and the herds of cows and sheep he kept on campus, McDonald was honored in 1939 with the dedication of Sam McDonald Road at Stanford and, in 1950, with the celebration of Sam McDonald Day.*

brief concession speech to the torchlit rally assembled at their home.

When Hoover left the White House the next year, Wilbur returned to his Stanford post to face the difficulty of guiding Stanford through the Depression years. Although the West Coast was not quite as devastated by the Depression as the East, homeless transients camped near Stanford along San Francisquito Creek. The job market was painfully tight for graduating seniors, and in 1933, Wilbur was forced to cut faculty salaries by 10 percent. College expenses were also going up, and a $1,000 relief drive was launched to raise funds to provide food, text-books, and clothes for cash-strapped students. Still, there were distractions from the gloom. The Varsity Theater in Palo Alto featured two movies for a quarter, starring film idols such as Joe E. Brown and Joan Blondell. Full-course French dinners for two at Bertrand's could be had for 25 cents. And on campus, ten-cent "Depression Dances" were organized as an inexpensive alternative to ritzy dates at the Mark Hopkins Hotel in San Francisco.

Serious scholarship and research advanced during the '30s, despite persistent budget problems. In 1934, Swiss physicist Felix Bloch (who would become Stanford's first Nobel Prize winner in 1952) arrived on campus, where he pursued his pioneering research on nuclear magnetic resonance. In 1937, brothers Russell and Sigurd Varian came to the University as unsalaried research associates. The two physicists began their collaboration with Stanford professor William W. Hansen that led to the invention of the klystron microwave tube—technology that spawned airborne radar technology and contributed to the development of the microelectronics industry. Two years later, two Stanford engineering graduates, William Hewlett and David Packard, launched their fledgling electronics business in a home garage with the support of electrical engineering professor Frederick E. Terman. New facilities were also constructed on campus. In 1936, the cornerstone was laid for Memorial Hall, in recognition of the World War I service of Stanford men and women. Frost Amphitheater was completed in 1937, and the following year a new School of Education building went up with money donated by retired education dean Ellwood P. Cubberley and his wife.

There were other important changes on the campus during the Depression years. The worsening economy had forced male enrollment down. Mainly to make up this enrollment deficit, the University in 1933 waived the cap on female enrollment—a limit that

Undergraduates study in Toyon Hall.

Collapse of the Boathouse

S TUDENTS JAMMED LAGUNITA
boathouse for the annual Junior Week
water carnival. During the 1938
festivities, the aging structure collapsed from
the weight of the spectators, pitching dozens
into the lake. Fortunately, there were no
injuries, and a new red-and-white boathouse
was built the next year.

Stoeffen Luisetti Moore Buin Turner Calderwood

From 1935 to 1938, the Stanford men's basketball team dominated the competition and revolutionized the game. Stanford's No. 7, Hank Luisetti, introduced innovations such as the one-handed shot and behind-the-back passing. He was named a First-Team All-America player three years in a row and twice named College Player of the Year.

Jane Stanford had set at 500 early in the University's history. The *Daily* declared the move "a depression-born blessing." At last, "women are no longer thought of as an addition but as a vital part of Stanford," announced dean of women Mary Yost (known to many as "the Holy Yost" because of her straitlaced reputation). Still, the University endeavored to restrict female enrollment to the ratio of 55 men to 45 women that had existed in 1899. Despite "the ratio"—as the proportionality rule was nicknamed—female enrollment immediately jumped to 800 in the fall quarter of 1933, and it more than tripled—to 1,722—by 1940.

Women's athletics enjoyed a somewhat freer environment in

the 1930s, too. In the late '20s, athletic competition, with its high emotions, had been considered inadvisable for women. Instead of competitive matches, Stanford's female athletes had participated in interschool "play days," whose motto was "play for play's sake" instead of "play to win." In the '30s, however, genuine competition was reinstated, and Stanford women athletes at last abandoned their impractical wool bloomers—"ominous, black, voluminous affairs," cringed the 1928 *Quad*—in favor of white cotton shorts and shirts, short socks and sneakers, or whatever suitable clothing they had on hand during the Depression.

Men's sports continued their achievements during the decade. In 1932 Stanford hosted the Olympic trials. That year, skinny Benjamin "Blazing Ben" Eastman, one of Stanford's greatest runners, smashed world records in six distances, and Bill Miller captured a gold medal in pole vaulting at the Los Angeles Olympic Games. In 1936, Stanford basketball player Angelo "Hank" Luisetti—called by some the greatest basketball player of his time—introduced the running one-handed jump shot during a game before a stunned crowd in New York's Madison Square Garden, shattering the opponents' forty-three-game winning streak and revolutionizing the game of basketball. And in football, Claude E. "Tiny" Thornhill coached a Cardinal football team whose players dubbed themselves the "Vow Boys," because in 1932 they had sworn never to be beaten by the University of Southern California (USC). It was a pledge they kept; between 1933 and 1935, the Vow Boys never lost a game to USC or Berkeley, took Stanford to the Rose Bowl three times, and achieved 20 shutouts in a thirty-one-game run. Stanford football's championship streak lasted past the '30s under coach Clark Shaughnessy—a man so intensely focused on the sport that he was once pulled over by traffic cops for driving while diagramming plays on his car windshield. Shaughnessy's 1940 "Wow Boys" picked up where the

From 1920 until the mid-1960s, the surviving wing of the Stanfords' Palo Alto residence—which was largely destroyed by the 1906 earthquake—served as the Children's Convalescent Home. At Con Home, as Stanford students affectionately called it, children recovering from surgery and illness benefited from a therapy of sunshine, fresh air, healthy food, and rest. Students raised funds and volunteered their labor every May during Con Home Week, repairing and sprucing up the facility and spending time with the young patients.

The Vow Boys:
Playing to Win

FROM 1933 TO 1936, the legendary "Vow Boys" made good on their pledge never to lose to the USC Trojans. In a 31-game stretch, they scored 20 shutouts and took Stanford to the Rose Bowl three times in a row—the first team ever to achieve that record. Although they lost the first two Rose Bowl contests—the first time to Columbia and the second time to Alabama—they capped their career by beating the SMU Mustangs 7-0 in the 1936 game. Five of the Vow Boys—Bill Corbus, Bobby Grayson, Bob "Horse" Reynolds, "Bones" Hamilton, and Monk Moscrip—were later honored as All-America players.

Students celebrate Back-to-the-Farm Days in November 1940.

Vow Boys had left off. Their revolutionary T-formation created a nationwide sensation, fueled a ten-game winning streak—including a Rose Bowl victory—and was eventually adopted by virtually every team in football.

By 1941, when Stanford University had passed its half-century mark, it had established itself as a respected regional university. Stanford had grown considerably since 1916, the beginning of Wilbur's presidency. Enrollment had climbed to 5,179 students from 2,199. The faculty had more than doubled to 295 from 118, and the number of graduate students had risen to 1,670 from 342, contributing to Stanford's growing lustre as a center of research. Stanford had, under

Wilbur's hand, achieved quality, stability, and reasonable growth. Edith Mirrielees, reflecting on Stanford's first 50 years, found cause to celebrate as well as much work to be done. "From the time of its opening," she observed, "Stanford had been moving step by step from its early status as a college and toward the university it aspired to be. By the '30s, Stanford scientists would have said the transition was completed…. The applied sciences, the professional schools, were strong, some of them outstanding." But, she cautioned, "the humanities were still pitted with weaknesses."

The responsibility for addressing these challenges would belong to the University's fourth president. Wilbur had reached the retirement age of 65 in 1940. At the board's request, however, he agreed to remain in his post until a new president was named. Meanwhile, war clouds were once again on the horizon. In 1940, all male students and professors age 21 to 30 registered for the nation's first peacetime military draft lottery. A 23-year-old resident of Mayfield Avenue named John Fitzgerald Kennedy—who was auditing business and political science classes at Stanford—drew draft number 18. On December 7, 1941, Pearl Harbor was attacked, and "so we were at war," *Daily* columnist Cheslie Saroyan wrote shortly after; despite the rumors and certainty that things would never be the same, "we tried to think that books and classes were important and we kept right on with our work."

STEEPLES OF
EXCELLENCE

 AMERICA'S ENTRY INTO WORLD WAR II BROUGHT a new seriousness of purpose to the Stanford campus. Instead of football games, dances, and debating matches, students found themselves preoccupied with air raid warnings and wartime obligations, from saving string to buying war bonds and conserving gasoline. Amid talk of sirens, bombers, and blackouts, the mood on campus was determined: "We must forget about ourselves and our troubles, and we must work, and work hard and suffer," the *Stanford Daily* urged. A new Civilian Defense Committee practiced blacking out the campus to avoid guiding enemy planes to nearby factories and Moffett Field.

Other defense measures had life-changing consequences for more than a dozen Stanford students and faculty members. In response to wartime fears and to Executive Order 9066 signed by President Roosevelt in February 1942, people of Japanese descent were forcibly evacuated from coastal areas, including Stanford University. On May 23, 1942, all Japanese Americans on campus were ordered transferred by train to the Santa Anita assembly center in southern California. The campus exodus was led by Yoshiro Oishi, president of the Japanese Student Association of Stanford University, and included Yamato Ichihashi, a 64-year-old Stanford alumnus and history professor who had taught at the University for three decades. "It was a most trying trip—hot, dirty and very uncomfortable," Ichihashi noted in a diary he kept of his internment experience. The meager food and "hideous sleeping place" that he and his wife were assigned at the Santa Anita center "made us feel very sad," he recorded. "It was an

Ray Lyman Wilbur poses with members of the Japanese Student Association.

awful comedown." Ichihashi and his family were confined there and at the Tule Lake and Amache internment centers, with tens of thousands of other Japanese Americans, until 1945.

The students and faculty who remained behind at Stanford soon found the campus dramatically transformed. "Our Ivory Towers of blissful isolation and protection, the sanctum of our Inner Quad," the *Daily* noted, "have been invaded by the startling and meaningful black-face headlines, the unavoidable exigencies of war, the khaki." By spring 1943, the University was swarming with soldier-students enrolled in special training courses. The uniformed trainees swelled Stanford's enrollment, straining physical and faculty resources to the limit. Classrooms were filled from 7:30 a.m. until 11:30 at night, and since many professors had left campus to serve in wartime jobs, the University called on others to fill the teaching gaps: the chaplain was enlisted to teach trigonometry, and a music professor was persuaded to teach engineering drawing. As civilian male enrollment plunged, women once again took over key Stanford positions. Jane Glasson became editor of the *Daily*, and for the first time, a woman—Janet McClanahan—was named president of the ASSU. In addition to their studies, women pledged to perform eight hours a month of "war work"—from rolling bandages to picking crops and collecting rubber tires. "Perhaps there will be no Yosemite weekends, no late City dates, no beach parties and no lavish formals," the *Daily* acknowledged. But "in spite of changes, Stanford has remained a kind of haven."

World War II had a dramatic impact on campus life. Students (top) pitched in to raise wartime funds in a "Dimes for Diplomas" campaign, and ASTP students trained for war service on the Stanford campus (above). As male enrollment dropped, women assumed campus leadership positions. Janet McClanahan, '44, (far right) was elected ASSU president; Marylou McClure, '46, (near right) took office as ASSU vice president.

Donald B. Tresidder, '19, MD '27, served as Stanford's president from 1943 until his death in 1948. A World War I aviator and president of the Yosemite Park and Curry Company, he headed Stanford's board of trustees before he was named president. Under Tresidder, Stanford created the first university planning office and streamlined administrative functions.

Even with the worries and disruptions of the war, Stanford in 1943 "was still a farm," remembered Mary Louise Tomblin, '46. "The campus was warm and pastoral. There was a smell of newly cut hay floating across Lake Lagunita and, although there were a few automobiles, hardly anyone had gas coupons. We bicycled to Searsville Lake and walked into town for movie dates…. It was a serious time, and yet it seemed so wonderful to live and learn on campus." It was during this short period of quiet and transition that Stanford-educated Donald Bertrand Tresidder, '19, MD '27, was named the University's fourth president. As head of Stanford's Board of Trustees, Tresidder had supervised the long search for a successor to Ray Lyman Wilbur—an effort frustrated by the wartime responsibilities of almost all the leading candidates.

At last, Tresidder himself was unanimously chosen by the board, and he assumed his duties as Stanford president in September 1943.

Robust and charismatic, "Uncle Don" considered himself a "students' president" and surrounded himself with undergraduates on vigorous Saturday morning hikes, trail breakfasts, and monthly open houses. The lanky, Indiana-born outdoorsman had never practiced medicine, nor was he an academic. Instead, Tresidder had pursued a successful commercial career as head of the Yosemite Park and Curry Company, and he brought businesslike reforms to Stanford's financial, administrative, planning, and fundraising activities. For the first time, the University president assumed full responsibility for nonacademic functions such as accounting, finance, maintenance, and student housing—duties that had previously been shared between the president and the business office. He also initiated a thoughtful, ongoing review of Stanford's physical plant. Under Tresidder, a planning office was organized in 1945 to look at land and facility use and Stanford's continuing

Female students fill the dining hall at Lagunita Court.

expansion—the first such function to be established at any university.

In the last years of the war, Stanford resembled a quiet women's college. Its tranquility was disrupted mainly by an increasing social schism between nonsorority students—more than 80 percent of all female undergraduates—and those who pledged sororities, which had become increasingly selective and competitive. After students voiced concerns about the growing polarization of the campus, sororities were banned in April 1944, a move that was generally applauded. After the war, the "women's college" atmosphere on campus was drastically transformed, however, by the flood of returning veterans funded by the "GI Bill," the Servicemen's Readjustment Act

Novelist Wallace Stegner established the Stanford Creative Writing Program in 1946. He directed it until 1971, the year he published his Pulitzer Prize-winning novel, Angle of Repose.

of 1944, and other government programs. The sudden invasion of discharged GIs, many of them married, sent Stanford enrollment soaring to 7,244 in 1946 and 8,213 in 1947, creating a critical shortage of campus housing. Some students made do in unheated, ill-ventilated quonset huts, and one married pair, Edith Mirrielees reported, was so desperate for shelter that they set up housekeeping in an unused chicken coop. To ease the pressure, Stanford took over Menlo Park's Dibble General Hospital from the army and transformed it into Stanford Village. Located three miles from campus on what was formerly the Timothy Hopkins estate, the makeshift but congenial compound offered apartments for 300 married couples and dormitory-style "barracks" for 1,500 others.

Despite scarce housing and crowded classrooms, the veterans applied themselves to school work with a vengeance. Older than most college undergraduates, they were nicknamed D.A.R.s—Damned Average Raisers—because they were so serious about their studies. "The chance for education being given them," Mirrielees observed, "they snatched at it, in a hurry to get what they had come for and to get as much of it as they could." The novelist Wallace Stegner, whom Tresidder had recruited from Harvard in 1945 to teach fiction and American literature, found himself suddenly "surrounded by GI students just out of the armed services, much more mature than the ordinary college student, with many more things to write, and with a sense of urgency brought on by three or four years of lost time in the army or navy." It was this extraordinary talent pool that inspired Stegner to establish the Stanford Creative Writing Program, whose alumni include authors Ken Kesey, Tillie Olsen, Larry McMurtry, Harriet Doerr, Raymond Carver, Alice Hoffman, and Robert Hass.

Scientific research at Stanford also received a postwar boost, thanks to a growing infusion of federal dollars for defense-related contracts. It was a trend that Tresidder hesitated to embrace, fearing that federal investment would have unwelcome strings attached. Nonetheless, he accurately predicted in 1946, "regardless of whether the prospect is wholly to our liking, the federal government will undoubtedly play a greater and greater role in higher education." To Tresidder, private-sector investment was more promising, and he actively sought to cultivate industry funding of campus research. In 1946 the University strengthened its ties with business by establishing the Stanford Research Institute (SRI), a nonprofit organization—affiliated with the University until 1970 and now known as SRI International—in which faculty members could apply their academic expertise to industry research and development.

Tresidder's efforts, however, were cut short. On January 28, 1948, the 53-year-old died suddenly in bed at the St. Regis Hotel in New York City, where he had planned to attend a university conference. It was not until the following year that the reins of the University were passed to Stanford's fifth president, J. E. Wallace Sterling, who took office on April 1, 1949. Formerly director of the Huntington Library and Art Gallery and a faculty member at the California Institute of Technology, the Canadian-born Sterling, 43, had earned his doctorate and taught history at Stanford. The university to which he now returned was poised for dynamic postwar growth but demoralized by the combined pressures of inflation, money shortages, and surging enrollment. Faculty members, Sterling noted, "were talking poor. For this there was justification," he recognized; "salaries were low; funds for library, for

During his 19 years as Stanford's fifth president, J. E. Wallace Sterling, PhD '38 (below left, with Herbert Hoover), focused on strengthening academic standards, expanding the faculty, and establishing Stanford as a premier research institution.

*A **Stanford** computer room in the 1950s.*

laboratory facilities, for research and publication and for travel were severely limited. Clearly more money was needed." To help improve campus morale, Sterling set out to engage the faculty in University affairs, actively seeking their ideas, involvement, and consensus. Optimistic and exuberant by nature, the large, affable Sterling quickly won the confidence of faculty and students. One undergraduate, a young Japanese woman named Fuji Imamura, never forgot her impression of Sterling when she met him at a reception for her graduating class in 1950. "I tell you," she remembered years later, "that I never shaked with any hands which were so large and thick and warm as our president's. Being wrapped up with his shovel-like hand, I could feel his understanding of human nature, wide mind and warm heart, and his strictness residing with kindness."

Sterling's most pressing priority was to raise Stanford's academic standards and reputation. Every emphasis, he insisted, "should be placed on efforts to build a faculty not merely of good men but of the best men, and to attract and sustain a student body capable of high academic performance." In this and virtually every other endeavor, he was brilliantly assisted by Frederick E. Terman, who was named Stanford's provost in 1954. An international authority on electronics, Terman had taught in Stanford's Department of Electrical Engineering in the 1930s, then served as head of the Harvard Radio Research Laboratory during World War II before returning to Stanford as dean of engineering in 1946. Terman shared Sterling's determination to raise the quality of Stanford's academics, contributing his own well-formulated ideas of what constituted a world-class university. "Academic prestige," Terman maintained, "depends upon high but narrow steeples of academic excellence.... Each steeple is formed by a small faculty group of experts in a narrow area of knowledge, and what counts is that the steeples be high for all to see." The goal at Stanford, he explained, would be "to build up a very great faculty strength in a few important but very narrow areas."

Sterling and Terman were clear about what needed to be done to build these "steeples of excellence" at Stanford. The University must "go for the best and pay what we need to pay," asserted Kenneth M. Cuthbertson, a Stanford vice president and architect of the University's postwar fundraising strategy. To do so, Stanford set out to raise the considerable revenues required to fund research programs and competitive faculty salaries. One key source of income throughout

Provost Frederick Terman (second from left) gathers *with President Sterling (second from right),* School of Engineering dean Joseph M. Pettit *(left), and* Board of Trustees president Richard W. Guggenhime *at the May 1965 dedication of the engineering lab named in Terman's honor.*

the 1950s continued to be federal grants and contracts, which jumped from nearly $1.4 million at the beginning of the decade to more than $10.5 million in 1959. Although the government contracts fueled Stanford's rise as a premier research institution, Sterling, like Tresidder, was cautious about the expanding federal role in higher education and expressed concerns about the "dangers of educational control." Government money, however, stimulated gifts from other outside sources—including foundations, industry, and private donors—and Sterling, an avid fundraiser, actively cultivated all these sources of support. By the end of the decade, foundation funding—not including major grants from the Ford Foundation—rose to more than $2 million a year from some $500,000 a year in the early 1950s. Corporate support climbed to more than $1.7 million, up from $158,000 over the same period, and total gifts soared to nearly $18.5 million from under $2 million in 1950—an achievement that placed Stanford second only to Harvard in the level of voluntary giving.

Between 1948 and 1958, Stanford had increased the size of its regular faculty by 48 percent, mainly as a result of these expanded streams of income. Stanford, Sterling explained, "used to offer salubrious climate and living conditions as part of a professor's reward.... Now," he quipped, "we meet the competition with dollars and throw in the sunshine." The University's new "steeples of excellence" were attracting national attention. Stanford's programs in engineering, physics, mathematics, and statistics had become among the very best in the country, and Stanford was competing nationally for graduate students in fields as diverse as English, psychology, physics, business, electronics, and law. In 1959, the University relocated the Medical School from San Francisco to the Stanford campus—a move that attracted two Nobel Prize winners in medicine, Arthur Kornberg and Joshua Lederberg, to the Stanford faculty. By the end of the decade, the faculty included 14 members of the National Academy of Sciences and four Nobel laureates, including physicist Willis E. Lamb, Jr., who was awarded the Nobel Prize for his discovery of a revised formula for the structure of the hydrogen atom. By 1959,

Left: *Stanford biology students in the early 1950s with a portion of the University's world-famous fish collection.*
Below: *Since 1960, Stanford biologists led by Paul Ehrlich have conducted a long-term study of bay checkerspot butterfly populations on Jasper Ridge. Their research has enhanced understanding of population dynamics as well as species conservation and restoration.*

Left: *Provost Frederick Terman* (right) *with electronic entrepreneurs David Packard* (far left), *and William Hewlett.*

Right: *Physics professor Felix Bloch* (left), *Stanford's first Nobel Prize winner, with William Webster Hansen, co-inventor of the klystron microwave tube, a device that helped launch the microelectronics industry.*

the University's rise prompted Wallace Stegner to declare in a letter to David Packard: "Stanford, which has always been a good university, is trembling on the brink of becoming one of the small number of great ones."

Stanford's electronic age also had its genesis during the postwar research boom of the 1950s. When Terman returned to Stanford's engineering department after the war, he actively attracted grants and faculty members to his department, establishing prestigious programs in such areas as solid-state electronics and microwave engineering. Today widely regarded as the "father of Silicon Valley," Terman also energetically cultivated Stanford's ties with industry, a synergy he had encouraged long before the war by organizing student field trips to electronics firms in the area. By the mid-1950s, Varian Associates, Eastman Kodak, Lockheed Aircraft's missile and space division,

Hewlett-Packard, and other technology firms were leasing land from Stanford in one of the first university research parks, and a reporter was already touting the Stanford area as a "great electronics center" and "a utopia of the electronics world."

The campus itself experienced a surge in construction under Sterling. More than 30 major building projects were completed, including the new Medical Center and Graduate School of Business, Meyer undergraduate library, science facilities, a Hoover Institution expansion, the Stanford Linear Accelerator Center, Bowman Alumni House, the Faculty Club, and Tresidder Memorial Union. Escondido Village was built for married students, and new dorms also went up, including Crothers Memorial Hall, Florence Moore, and Wilbur Hall.

Undergraduate education in the 1950s was making strides as well. The expanded faculty meant smaller classes and the chance for students to associate more closely with their instructors. A wide-ranging study of the undergraduate program, commenced in 1954, resulted in a new curricular focus on "general studies" throughout the four undergraduate years. By 1959, as a result of more demanding admissions requirements, Stanford's student body included the fourth-highest number of National Merit Scholars in the country. And in a move to broaden the experience and perspectives of undergraduates, the Stanford Overseas Campuses program was organized. Stanford-in-Germany—Stanford's first overseas center and the first European branch of any major American university—opened outside Stuttgart in 1958, followed by campuses in France, Italy, Austria, and Great Britain. By the late 1960s, the program was so successful that more than half of all Stanford students studied abroad at some point during their undergraduate years.

Above: *The Dish, a 150-foot radio telescope in the Stanford foothills, has been a campus landmark since it was built in the 1960s to explore scattering properties of earth's ionosphere. SRI International owns and maintains the Dish today, and it is used by Stanford's Space, Telecommunications, and Radioscience (STAR) Laboratory for radio spectrum research.*
Right: *A "stop the bomb" protest on campus in the early 1960s.*

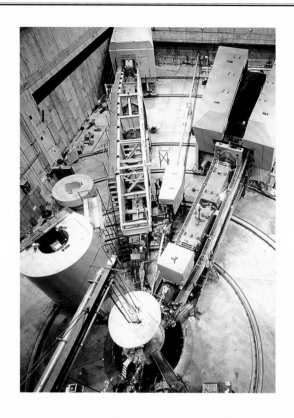

SLAC: Center of High-Energy Research

T HE STANFORD LINEAR ACCELERATOR
Center (SLAC) is a national laboratory
founded in 1962 to conduct basic research
in elementary particle physics. Its most familiar
landmark is the linac (shown right, in 1967)—
a 2-mile-long linear accelerator, completed in
1966, that produces high-energy electron and
positron beams.

Above: In 1990, Stanford's Richard Taylor and
MIT's Jerome E. Friedman and Henry W.
Kendall won the Nobel Prize in physics for pioneering research they conducted on these large
magnetic spectrometers at SLAC, work that
probed the deep inelastic scattering of electrons.

Reverend Martin Luther King, Jr., spoke at Stanford in 1964 and (above) *in 1967, a year before his death.*

On the home campus, the '50s were comparatively calm, despite the escalating Cold War, McCarthyism, and the Korean conflict. Students entertained themselves with television, pizza parties, and spelunking through the underground steam tunnels that carried hot water around campus. Special rules for women stayed in effect throughout the decade, recalled Lynda Lytle Holmstrom, '61—"curfew; sign-out sheets; weekly dress-up dinner; skirts a must for the Quad; and, if unmarried, residence on campus in single-sex dorms." Separate men's and women's rooting sections filled the stands at football games—the women in red skirts and the men in red rooters' caps—and the Stanford band paraded in snappy military-style uniforms topped with tall plumed hats. In 1951, Charles A. "Chuck" Taylor was named national football coach of the year after taking Stanford to the Rose Bowl. Stanford athletes also put on gold-winning performances in the Olympic Games. At the 1952 Olympics in Helsinki, Bob Mathias won his second gold medal in the decathlon and became the first athlete to compete in the Rose Bowl and the Olympics in the same year. Other Stanford Olympians captured gold medals in crew in 1956, 1960 and 1964.

After the inward-looking '50s, the early '60s saw the beginnings of a growing restlessness on campus. Faculty members were migrating to Stanford from other universities, and enrollment, particularly of graduate students, continued to expand, swelling by some 40 percent between 1948 and 1968. As Stanford grew and became more diverse, change was in the wind, stirred by the emerging civil rights movement and the war in Vietnam. In 1963, the posting of yellow-and-black civil defense signs identifying newly stocked campus fallout-shelters sparked Stanford's first political demonstration of the era, a peaceful twenty-four-hour vigil. Then, in April 1964, Reverend Martin Luther King, Jr., gave the first of two addresses at Stanford. The speech inspired some 40 Stanford students—the largest contingent from any university—to head east to Mississippi as civil rights workers in the historic "freedom summer," a Peace Corps-like mobilization in which volunteers staffed voter registration programs, "freedom schools," and other community-based projects.

By 1966, antiwar protests were spreading across the country, and the political climate at Stanford had become increasingly charged. Activist students challenged university policies on issues such as defense research, ROTC, and free speech and staged the first campus sit-in, a three-day occupation of President Sterling's office. The next year, two thousand protesters took part in a massive, all-night peace vigil at Memorial Church. After the assassination of Martin

After King's assassination in April 1968, members of the Black Student Union (BSU) protested on campus, demanding higher minority enrollment at Stanford.

Luther King, Jr., in April 1968, student militancy grew even more strident. Then-provost Richard Lyman was giving a speech at Memorial Auditorium when members of the Black Student Union (BSU) surrounded him on stage, demanding increased minority enrollment, hiring, and financial aid. "Stanford was a stubborn mule then," remembered Leo Bazile, '71, former head of the BSU. "We had to pick up a stick and hit the mule between the eyes to get its attention." In response, Sterling and Lyman agreed to double minority-group enrollment by the next academic year. It was time, Lyman noted, "to set an institution, for which we cared deeply, on the road toward diversity after many decades of injustice and exclusion."

Despite the sit-ins, demonstrations, and civil disobedience, academic life thrived at Stanford in the '60s. The well-funded faculty recruitment efforts continued. "Along with dollars came scholars: Stanford is raiding blue-chip faculties all over the East," *Time* magazine reported in 1961. There were groundbreaking academic achievements throughout the decade, including physicist Robert Hofstadter's Nobel Prize for research on the structure of atomic nuclei; Nobel laureate Arthur Kornberg's pioneering genetic work at Stanford as head of the new Department of Biochemistry; the first adult human heart transplant in the United States, performed by Dr. Norman Shumway at the Stanford Medical Center; and the publication of biology professor Paul Ehrlich's bestselling book *The Population Bomb*.

Financially, the University was also on sound footing. In 1959, the "Red Book"—a long-range study of Stanford's academic and financial goals—helped the University secure a $25 million Ford Foundation grant, the largest ever awarded to any university. During the early '60s, this funding served as seed money for the ambitious PACE campaign (Plan of Action for a Challenging Era), which raised a

Left: *Ken Kesey, author of* One Flew Over the Cuckoo's Nest *and* Sometimes a Great Notion, *enrolled in Stanford's Creative Writing Program in 1958. In 1964, he set off around the country in a Day-Glo-painted school bus with a group of counterculture adventurers called the Merry Pranksters.* **Above:** *Students at Stanford in the 1960s.*

record $114 million for Stanford in three years. By 1968—driven by aggressive faculty recruiting, fundraising, and the surge in postwar government and industry contracts—Stanford had transformed itself from a good regional institution into one of the most prestigious research universities in the world.

After 19 years as president, however, Sterling was "aging and tired," Lyman recalled, and distressed by the increasing divisiveness at Stanford. "Institutional loyalties," Lyman noted, were "strained by the unprecedented waves of dissension and rebellion on campus. Consensus as to the nature and purposes of a university were simply impossible for a time." Then, in July 1968, two months before his planned retirement, Sterling had his office gutted by an arson fire that destroyed many of his books, paintings, personal papers, and mementos. In September, as planned, he stepped down from the presidency and was named the University's chancellor for life. "I have always thought it particularly poignant that towards the close of 'the Sterling Years,' Wally had to face so much damage to the climate in which the University had flourished," Lyman reflected years later. "Fortunately, he lived to see all that change, too, and to find himself reestablished in the overwhelming majority of Stanford hearts and minds as the heroic figure who had led the University to, and then over, that famous 'edge of greatness.'"

STANFORD: PORTRAIT OF A UNIVERSITY

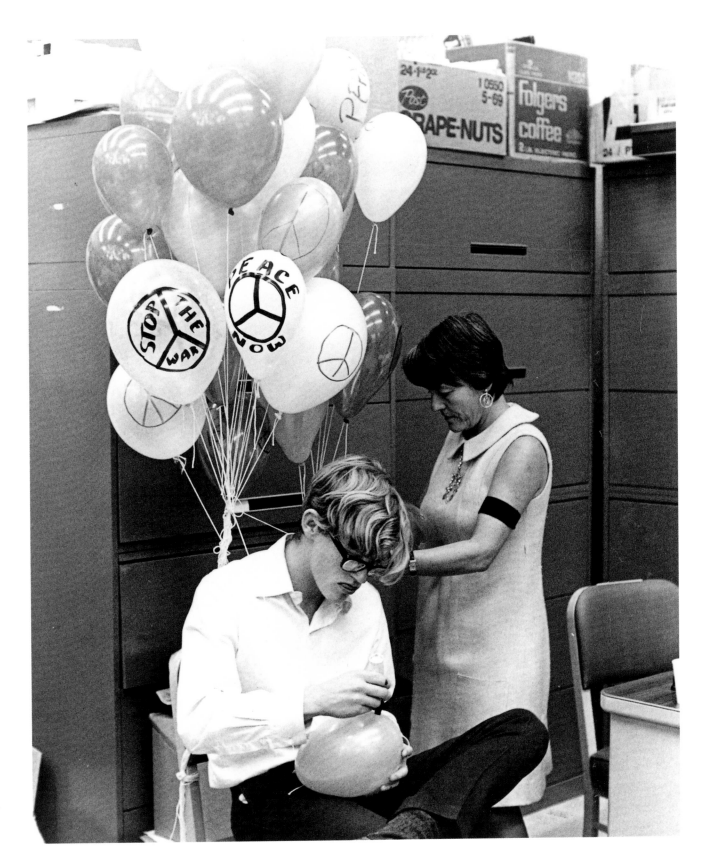

HIGHER HORIZONS

STANFORD: PORTRAIT OF A UNIVERSITY

Preceding pages: *Hoover Tower and Lake Lagunita.*
Left: *Police were frequently called to campus as antiwar protests turned violent.*
Below: *Provost Richard Lyman addresses a crowd of student demonstrators.*

T FELL TO STERLING'S SUCCESSOR, NATIONALLY respected chemist Kenneth Pitzer, to guide Stanford through the near-chaos that shook the nation's campuses in the late 1960s and early '70s. It was a task some of Pitzer's students compared to "jumping into boiling oil." The 54-year-old Pitzer had served successful terms as dean of UC-Berkeley's College of Chemistry and president of Rice University, but little in his experience prepared him for the upheaval that was engulfing Stanford and other major universities. "It was," his provost Richard Lyman later remarked, "pretty much a descent into hell between 1968 and 1970."

As the war in Vietnam intensified, Stanford students' protests against the war, ROTC, and defense-related research escalated from peaceful sit-ins to increasingly disruptive and violent confrontations. In those divisive years, when student demonstrations became steadily more militant, there was a sense, Lyman recalled, "that things were up for grabs and that the future was just very full of risk. It's very hard to convey that to young people today. They can't imagine a campus where you stop replacing broken glass that gets broken faster than you can replace it."

Campus insurrections reached a new level in the spring of

1969, when police were called to Stanford for the first time to quell a student occupation of Encina Hall and used tear gas to clear hundreds of protesters from the Stanford Research Institute. Violence raged across the campus the next spring, following the invasion of Cambodia and the killing of four students by National Guardsmen at Kent State University. Decades of one scholar's research were destroyed in an arson attack on the Center for Advanced Study in Behavioral Sciences, and rock-throwing protesters battled police riot squads in White Plaza. In April and May 1970, police were summoned to the campus 13 times, and at least 20 students and 45 officers were injured in the conflicts.

Left: *In 1969, campus militants ransacked the Stanford Bookstore.*
Above: *The following year, student activists occupied the Old Union to protest military training on campus.*

The disruption "was just sort of impossible to stop," Pitzer acknowledged in an interview years later.

Sprawling and isolated, Stanford was an especially tempting target for radicals who sought to use deliberate violence as a way to bring military research to a halt. In their view, according to a *Daily* writer, "the university (and especially Stanford) supplied the brain power necessary to make the 'military-industrial complex' work." If they could shut down Stanford and other universities, they hoped, "they could force the nation to stop its capitalist and racist actions."

Frustrated by the violence and disruption, Pitzer announced his resignation, effective on September 1, 1970, and Richard W. Lyman was named Stanford's seventh president. Forthright and articulate, the Philadelphia-born Lyman was already well known to Stanford students. An historian educated at Swarthmore and Harvard, he had taught at Stanford since 1958, and as provost he was admired for his tough-minded stewardship during the troubled years since 1967. His selection was welcomed by many on campus as "a steadying force," *Daily* writer Marshall Kilduff noted at the time; Lyman was widely respected for his "sharply incisive tongue and principled, rigorous mind." He quickly drew clear lines between activities that would be tolerated and those that had no place in the University community. Under Lyman, Stanford articulated a firm policy "that sit-ins were an unacceptable form of doing business in a university. And when they happened, they would be brought to a close as soon as it was possible to do it safely," recalled Robert Rosenzweig, who served as a vice provost during Lyman's term.

The worst incidents, however, were still to come. A sit-in at Stanford Hospital resulted in at least 22 injuries and 23 arrests. Campus buildings were sprayed with political graffiti, their windows smashed by rocks and railroad spikes. Associate professor of English Bruce Franklin was dismissed from the Stanford faculty

Below: *Protesters make* Daily *headlines in May 1970.*
Bottom: *In this telegram, students who occupied Encina Hall in May 1969 stated their antiwar demands.*

for calling for "a people's war on campus" and inciting student violence. Lyman's office was ripped by an explosion, the Junipero House lounge in Wilbur Hall was gutted by a suspected arson fire, and two students were wounded by an unknown gunman in a student-police clash near Meyer Library.

In those crisis-filled months, Lyman acknowledged, there was a "sense of near-desperation that many of us felt." Still, to keep lines of communication open, he regularly fielded questions on the air at the campus radio station, KZSU—a move, he reflected, that "made it much more difficult for the radical movement to argue that you couldn't get an answer out of the administration." Lyman's unflinching leadership earned him widespread respect. As the *Daily* commented, he "firmly managed the University during a time when attacks from within and without, budget cuts, a lack of direction, and a tension and polarization...have left it vulnerable and often defenseless."

Kenneth Pitzer, Stanford's president from 1968–70, talked with student protesters outside his office in 1968.

Student activism was not the only challenge Lyman faced. Though federal support of higher education had begun to shrink by 1967 and 1968, the University's expenses were continuing to grow rapidly. Cutbacks had been put in place beginning in the late '60s, and Lyman decided to forgo a traditional inauguration in consideration of Stanford's budget problems. Avoiding a "downward spiral of ever-increasing deficits" became one of his chief priorities. For the first time, under Lyman, the University began computer modeling of various financial scenarios to bring the budget into balance. At the same time, Stanford actively sought alumni and foundation support for the endowment and capital improvements. This was a huge challenge, given the displeasure of many alumni with the campus protests and Lyman's 1972 decision to end Stanford's use of the "Indian" mascot—a symbol many increasingly criticized as a stereotyped racial image. Despite these major obstacles, the University launched an

Right: *After 42 years as Stanford's mascot, the "Indian" symbol was retired by the ASSU Senate in 1972, following President Richard Lyman's recommendation.*

audacious "Campaign for Stanford" in 1972 with a $300 million goal, the highest target set by any university. "The feeling was that we couldn't afford to let alumni disaffection get in the way," Lyman explained. Even though the University, he granted, seemed to be so at war with itself that it was

alienating outside support, Stanford "had to do as much of what it normally does as possible without being deterred." In spite of the considerable obstacles, the campaign exceeded its fundraising objectives, bringing in a total of $304 million by 1977.

From the beginning of his presidency, Lyman also was determined to keep Stanford in the first rank of American universities by continuing to recruit top scholars and strengthening departments and faculties campuswide. "This university counts for something because it has moved far and fast," he told the Academic Council in October 1970. "It is going to go on moving," he pledged, "and we are not going to be distracted by destructive attacks." The fundraising campaign raised the number of endowed professorships from 49 to 125, and throughout the '70s, academic achievements continued at a rapid pace. Two faculty members claimed Nobel Prizes: chemistry professor Paul J. Flory for his research on polymers, and physics professor Burton Richter for his discovery of a new type of elementary particle. Pulitzer Prizes were awarded to Carl Degler and Wallace Stegner, and six Stanford scholars received National Medals of Science: Paul Flory; Frederick Terman; physics professor Wolfgang Panofsky; chemistry professors Henry Taube and Carl Djerassi; and George Dantzig, professor of operations research and computer science.

Top: When Sweden's King Carl XVI Gustaf (center) visited Stanford in 1984, the University's 10 living Nobel laureates met together for the first time: (from left) chemistry professor Henry Taube, physics professors Arthur Schawlow and Robert Hofstadter, chemistry professors Paul Flory and Paul Berg, physics professors Burton Richter and William Shockley, economics professor Kenneth Arrow, chemistry professor Linus Pauling, and biochemistry professor Arthur Kornberg. **Above:** *Nobel Prize medallion.*

In 1975, exiled Soviet writer and Nobel laureate Alexander Solzhenitsyn studied Hoover Institution archives to research his history of Russia in 1917. Before he left Stanford, he was named an honorary fellow of the Hoover Institution.

Stanford geophysicist Allan V. Cox garnered the prestigious Vetlesen Prize for his work in paleomagnetic research and plate tectonics. And Stanford genetics professor Stanley Cohen—together with lab technician Annie Chang and Herbert Boyer of UC-San Francisco—launched the biotechnology industry by developing a revolutionary method for transplanting genes from one species to another.

Curricular reform was also high on Lyman's agenda—especially after the campus violence and upheaval ended suddenly and unexpectedly in 1972. The war and the draft, at last, were winding down, and nationwide, students were turning away from disruptive civil disobedience. Civility returned in part, Lyman surmised, because "it was pretty obvious that the movement," with its increasing violence, "was headed in a direction that was not acceptable." Instead of riots and confrontations in the spring of 1972, there was a campus-wide spring cleaning. And Lyman was at last able to begin turning much of his attention from crisis management to long-range academic issues, particularly the debate over undergraduate requirements. Since the late '60s, he explained, "there was a feeling that required courses were constricting for faculty and students. But I felt that it was important to emerge from college with a sense of where you came from. I spent a lot of time in the last half of my presidency working with faculty committees to try to restore meaningful requirements." Among his most significant reforms was the Western Culture Program, an array of interdepartmental courses with a common reading list and purpose, which became a freshman requirement in 1980. Stanford's Institute for Research on Women and Gender was founded, and another interdisciplinary course of studies, the Human Biology Program, flourished under Lyman. Financed by a $1.9 million grant awarded by the Ford Foundation in 1970, human biology—which combined biological, medical, and behavioral sciences—was the first program of its kind to be offered by any university.

The 1970s also saw the reinvigoration of Stanford sports—a trend that had begun in the late '60s after a discouraging, decade-long slump. Men's tennis coach Dick Gould recalled that in the mid-1960s, many believed "that Stanford was a loser athletically. The football team had been having its problems"—winning only 38 out of a hundred games between 1958 and 1968—"and things were at a low ebb. People said that you couldn't win at Stanford, that you couldn't combine athletics and academics." In the early '70s, however, the Stanford football squad, led by Heisman Trophy-winning quarterback Jim Plunkett, disproved that thesis and reclaimed its reputation with a powerful passing game. Plunkett and his successor, quarterback Don Bunce, won back-to-back Rose Bowls in 1971 and 1972—the first Rose Bowl victories since

Below: *The birth control pill was invented by a scientific team led by organic chemist and Stanford faculty member Carl Djerassi, winner of the National Medal of Science and the National Medal of Technology.*

Below: *President Richard Lyman in 1973.*
Right: *In 1980, Stanford biology professor and former Food and Drug Administration commissioner Donald Kennedy became Stanford's eighth president.*

1941—and other sports gained new momentum, too. Under Gould, the Stanford tennis team won six NCAA championships between 1973 and 1981. And with coach Dante Dettamanti, who arrived in 1977, the Stanford water polo squad continued the championship record started by coach Art Lambert the year before—capturing three NCAA championships and winning 90 percent of their games from 1977 until 1982.

Seeds also were sown in the '70s for a powerful women's sports program. The government passed Title IX of the Federal Education Amendments Act in 1972—landmark legislation that banned gender discrimination at any school receiving federal funding. "Before Title IX," remembered Anne Gould, '71, an instructor in Stanford's tennis program, "women's sports were treated like P.E. classes. The women's tennis team could only practice twice a week and never had new balls or any budget for travel." As one of the first steps toward parity, the men's and women's athletic and physical education departments were merged in 1975 to form the department of athletics, physical education and recreation, and women athletes were offered athletic grants-in-aid for the first time. "Suddenly," Gould said, "we had funding for equipment, travel, scholarships. For all women athletes at Stanford, Title IX vastly improved opportunities and the quality of play."

The '70s ended with a change of leadership at Stanford. In 1980, Lyman elected to leave Stanford to head the Rockefeller Foundation in New York, and Provost Donald Kennedy, a Harvard-educated biologist and former commissioner of the Food and Drug Administration, was named Stanford University's eighth president. Enthusiastic and open-minded, Kennedy—a popular biology professor who had chaired Stanford's department of biological sciences from 1965 to 1972—quickly set out to forge strong relationships with students, serving as a freshman advisor and inviting undergraduates along on bird-watching excursions and early-morning

A Different Drum: The LSJUMB

T HE LELAND STANFORD JUNIOR
University Marching Band (LSJUMB)
has come a long way since the 1890s (top
left), when it was founded. Once a precision
marching band clad in military-style uniforms,
playing rousing renditions of the classics, the
Stanford Band changed forever in 1963, when
musical arts doctoral student Arthur P. Barnes
took over as director. Abandoning traditional
John Philip Sousa arrangements, Barnes, who
retired in 1997, determined to make the
LSJUMB "the world's largest rock and roll
band." Storming the field in red blazers and
fishing hats, the student-run Band has ever
since delighted and alarmed audiences with its
raucous misbehavior and often controversial
musical selections and formations.

In 1972, a milestone year, the Band for
the first time admitted women to its ranks
and debuted its trademark anthem "All Right
Now" (originally recorded by the British
rock band Free). A decade later, in the 1982
Big Game, the Band made football history in
"The Play" (bottom right). Prematurely
assuming a 20-19 Stanford victory, Band
members flooded the end zone with four
seconds still remaining in the game—causing
the Cal Bears to pull off an astonishing
five-lateral kickoff return and game-winning
touchdown through a red-coated mass of
trumpets, tubas, and trombones.

Above: Band members and Stanford Dollies in
the mid-1960s.

Top right: The LSJUMB rushes the field in
the late 1980s.

Far right: The Band's incomparable mascot,
the Tree, joined the LSJUMB in the late
1970s.

runs to "the Dish," the radio telescope nestled in the Stanford foothills. One of his first priorities was to urge a return to teaching as the University's main focus. "The fragile relationship between students and faculty…experienced serious damage in the late 1960s and early '70s," he noted in his inaugural address. "The events of the 1960s left relatively untouched the fellowship of the laboratory bench, the dissertation conference, and the review journal. But faculty participation in residential education, in advising, and in more casual voluntary relationships with students—these were frequent casualties." To renew their ties with students, he urged faculty members to engage in teaching-related research and to mentor students in honors theses and other independent investigations. Stanford must, he declared, "strengthen and preserve, in the midst of one of the world's greatest research universities, an undergraduate college that is selective, distinctive, rigorous, and inspiring."

Kennedy also helped to build an increasingly multicultural undergraduate curriculum—reflecting, in part, the changing nature of the student body. In the seven-year period from 1984 to 1991, the composition of the freshman class changed dramatically, with the proportion of African-American, Asian-American, Mexican-American, and Native American students climbing from 27 percent to more than 40 percent. As Stanford more actively sought racial, economic, and geographic diversity, there were also academic changes, including new courses in gender studies and American and world cultures. The Western culture requirement was expanded into Cultures, Ideas and Values, with a curriculum that included non-Western European texts.

Kennedy also actively encouraged student involvement in public service. As he explained in a 1983 letter to Stanford alumni, "We want to challenge students to expand their view of entrepreneurship beyond the profit sector, to include the search for creative solutions to pressing social problems." His emphasis on public service, Kennedy recalled, was partly a response to "the dreadful way in which the attitudes of undergraduates in the early 1980s were being reported

Right: *A Native American dancer at the 1990 annual Stanford Powwow, one of the largest Indian gatherings on the West Coast.*

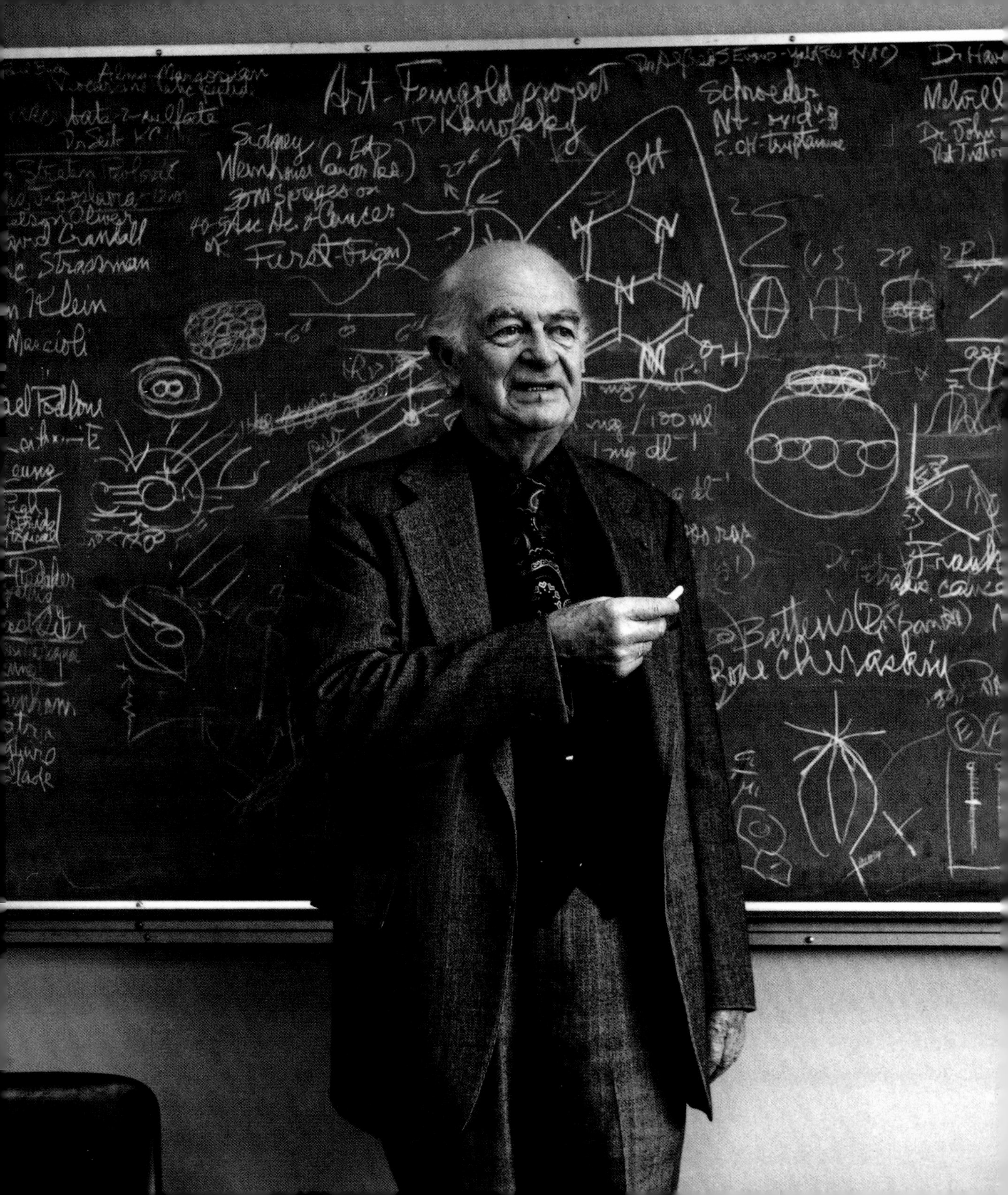

Nobel laureates on the Stanford faculty have included the late Linus Pauling (left), a Stanford chemistry professor from 1969 to 1973, who won the 1954 Nobel Prize in Chemistry for his research into chemical bonds and the 1962 Nobel Peace Prize for his efforts to end nuclear testing; Arthur Kornberg (below), professor emeritus of biochemistry and cowinner of the 1959 Nobel Prize in Medicine for his achievements in synthesizing DNA; physics professor Douglas Osheroff (bottom left), cowinner of the 1996 Nobel Prize in Physics for discovering superfluidity in helium-3; and physics professor Steven Chu (bottom right), cowinner of the 1997 Nobel Prize in Physics for his research in the field of laser cooling and trapping.

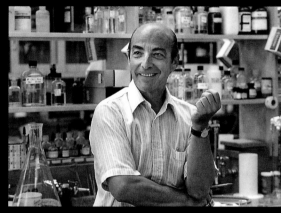

to the American people. Students were said to be motivated by visions of economic success and to lack any sense of obligation to society. They were caricatured as careerists, disinterested not only in their fellow human beings but in literature, the arts, indeed in anything apparently not directly related to achieving the Good Life." Although Kennedy disagreed with the critiques, he saw the importance of creating "some real outlets for our own undergraduates to express other values." In 1984, he established the Public Service Center—renamed the Haas Center for Public Service in 1989—as a clearinghouse to match student interests with volunteer needs in the community. As a result of this heightened focus, student involvement in community activities at Stanford rose from 40 percent in 1984 to 70 percent in 1992.

Left: *In 1989, "Roble refugees" squeezed into temporary quarters in Branner Hall while earthquake reinforcements were completed at Roble. The seismic upgrading was finished shortly before the Loma Prieta earthquake.*

Above: *In 1993, Amy Biehl, '89, was killed in an outbreak of racial violence in South Africa, where she was working as a Fulbright Fellow. In 1998, a summer fellowship was established in her memory for Stanford students volunteering in South Africa.*

Stanford also reached new levels of academic excellence. Nobel Prizes were awarded to five Stanford scholars between 1980 and 1991—biochemistry professor Paul Berg for his research on nucleic acids, physics professor Arthur Schawlow for research in laser spectroscopy, chemistry professor Henry Taube for his work on electronic transfer reactions, Business School professor emeritus William Sharpe for his work in corporate finance and financial economics, and physics professor Richard Taylor for his discovery of quarks. Chemistry professors Richard N. Zare and Harden M. McConnell were awarded the National Medal of Science. Many Stanford scholars also helped shape national policy: more than twenty Hoover Institution scholars and Stanford professors were appointed to advisory posts in President Ronald Reagan's administration.

Stanford alumni also achieved exceptional distinction. In 1983, astronaut Sally Ride, '73, MS '75, PhD '78, became the first American woman in space. Two years earlier, another alumna, Sandra Day O'Connor, '50, LLB '52, entered history as the first woman justice on the U.S. Supreme Court. In 1986, her Stanford Law School classmate William Rehnquist was appointed chief justice, and in 1988, they were joined on the Supreme Court bench by a third Stanford alumnus,

The Hub of Silicon Valley

E VER SINCE ENGINEERING professor Frederick Terman forged Stanford's first links with electronics companies in the 1930s, the University has been an incubator for fast-growing Silicon Valley firms, from Hewlett-Packard to Cisco, Sun Microsystems, Silicon Graphics, and Yahoo!

At Stanford, the boundaries between academics and industry are fluid. In a class, for example, taught by industrial engineering professor Tom Byers (top), students work as interns at startup technology companies. In 1982, Scott McNealy, MBA '80 (middle), cofounded Sun Microsystems with fellow Stanford students Andreas Bechtolsheim and Vinod Khosla; the company's name is an acronym for Stanford University Network. John Morgridge (bottom), MBA '57, chairs Cisco Systems, launched in 1984 by Stanford computing directors Sandy Lerner and Leonard Bosack. Morgridge, in turn, has come back to campus to teach a course for Stanford MBA candidates on "Entrepreneurship: Formation of New Ventures."

Anthony M. Kennedy, '58. Stephen Breyer, '59, was named a Supreme Court justice in 1994. Beginning in the early 1980s, Stanford faculty, students, and alumni also began providing much of the talent and vision that fueled the growth of Silicon Valley and led to the creation of companies such as Cisco Systems, Silicon Graphics, and Sun Microsystems.

Throughout the '80s and early '90s, Stanford sports teams excelled across the board. In 1986, Stanford boasted the greatest number of individual champions in Division I of the NCAA, ranked in the top 10 nationally in 16 sports, and held national championships in four. Stanford's baseball team won the College World Series in both 1987 and 1988, and women's sports achieved national prominence, capturing NCAA titles in swimming in 1983, basketball in 1990 and 1992, and volleyball in 1993. Stanford Stadium also served as the site of major national and international sports events during the '80s, hosting nine Olympic soccer matches in 1984 and Super Bowl XIX in 1985—the first one ever to be held in a college football stadium.

Across the campus, the University's physical facilities were renovated and expanded with help from funds provided by a $1.27 billion "Centennial Campaign," a five-year fundraising drive—again, the largest ever attempted by any university. The campaign increased Stanford's endowment by $343 million and exceeded its ambitious goal by $170 million. New campus construction included the Lucile Packard Children's Hospital, Governor's Corner residence halls, Braun Music Center, and the Beckman Center for Molecular and Genetic Medicine, as well as a major seismic upgrading of Roble Hall.

But just weeks after the Roble reinforcement was completed—on October 17, 1989—Stanford was rocked by the second major earthquake in its history, a 7.1 temblor that collapsed a chimney of the Old Chemistry Building, cracked the archways of the Inner Quad, tumbled thousands of books from the shelves of Green and Meyer libraries, and caused serious structural damage to fifteen row houses, the west wing of Green Library, Geology Corner, the museum, the Graduate School of Business, and Memorial Church. Amazingly, there

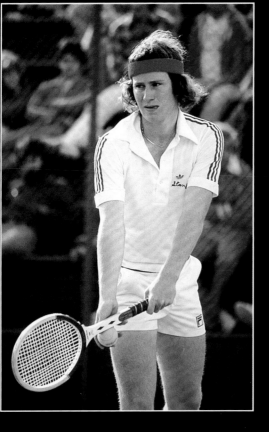

Thanks to the powerful performance of its sports teams, Stanford's overall athletic program was named the best in the country in 1995, 1996, 1997, 1998 and 1999. Stanford Champions have included Jennifer Azzi (left), *two-time women's basketball All-American; John McEnroe* (above), *the world's top-ranked tennis player from 1980-84; 1997 Masters champion golfer Tiger Woods* (top right); *1992 Stanford Olympic swimmers* (from left) *Angie Wester-Krieg, Lea Loveless, Summer Sanders, Jenny Thompson and coach Richard Quick* (center right); *and Kristin Folkl* (bottom right), *one of the top athletes in Stanford history, who won All-America honors in both volleyball and basketball.*

Above: *The 1989 Loma Prieta earthquake damaged 242 buildings at Stanford. One of the hardest-hit structures was the west wing of Green Library, which cost some $35 million to repair.*
Right: *Debris filled Memorial Church after the quake.*

were no deaths or serious injuries on campus. However, many students were forced to evacuate their living quarters—camping out in dorm lounges, on lawns, and in the shelter of the Old Pavilion. "People from dorms and houses that were damaged slept in our lounge for days," recalled Katherine Toy, '91, MA '95, a resident of the refurbished Roble, which survived the quake relatively well.

The University community, for the most part, took the disaster in stride. Hundreds of campus residents volunteered for earthquake relief work, helping out both on campus and in hard-hit towns such as Watsonville and Santa Cruz. Classrooms and offices were hastily relocated, and Stanford was almost fully operational a week after the quake. Nonetheless, total damage was estimated at more than $150 million, and reconstruction of the museum and library continued for a decade.

The trauma of the earthquake was soon followed by another episode that painfully shook Stanford. In 1990, allegations were made that the University had overcharged the government for indirect costs associated with federal research contracts at Stanford. The accusations attracted enormous publicity and scrutiny—despite the fact that ultimately, in 1994, the federal government concluded that Stanford had engaged in no fraud, misrepresentation, or other wrongdoing with respect to agreements, costs, submissions or claims. Before that conclusion was reached, in the fall of 1991, Kennedy decided that he had become "more of a lightning rod than my university needed" and announced that he would resign as president in August 1992. "It is very difficult," he explained, "for a person identified...with a

Above: *Exercising global spirit by the Quad.*
Right: *Students enjoying the Stanford sunshine.*

problem to be a spokesman for its solution." According to dean of students Michael Jackson, Kennedy had been an "inspirational leader" whose vision had resulted in great changes in the diversity and character of the University. "Donald Kennedy will be missed," the *Stanford Daily* stated. "The able and affable administrator has presided over an impressive decade in Stanford's history: one in which the University grew to international prestige and was the center of some of higher education's most vigorous debates."

Kennedy's successor—Stanford University's ninth president—was 54-year-old Gerhard Casper. A constitutional law expert known for his scholarship and wit, Casper had served as provost and law school dean at the University of Chicago. Born in Hamburg, Germany, where he received his undergraduate law degree, he had earned a master of laws degree from Yale and a doctorate from the University of Freiburg. At Stanford, Casper promised early in his tenure to lead a campus-wide dialogue about the character and direction of the University at the beginning of its second century. "One of my highest priorities," he explained in 1994, "…has been to engage my faculty colleagues, our students, the staff, the trustees, and the University's alumni and friends in a review of our institutional priorities—particularly our curriculum and policies related to research and teaching.… What kind of institution are we? What should we be? What should we do? How should we do it?"

Part of that inward look, inevitably, involved a reexamination of Stanford's fiscal and academic priorities. During Casper's first years as president, he addressed the financial challenges presented

Celebrating the Centennial

T HOUSANDS GATHERED TO
mark Stanford's hundredth
birthday at the University's
centennial celebration in 1991. The
four-day event included parades,
roundtable discussions, hundreds of
classes, and addresses by former
Secretary of State George Shultz,
Canadian prime minister Brian
Mulroney, and Mexican president
Carlos Salinas de Gortari.
Following pages: Fireworks lit the
sky during the centennial event's
"Stadium Spectacular."

Mae Jemison, '77, the first African-American woman in space, served as a mission specialist aboard the space shuttle Endeavour *in 1992.*

by earthquake recovery and lowered government research reimbursement. Working closely with provost Condoleezza Rice, he streamlined administrative procedures, pared budgets, and set out aggressively to raise additional funds. In 1993, he also launched a comprehensive review of Stanford's undergraduate curriculum. "I think Stanford has had a better record than many universities in terms of faculty commitment to undergraduate education," Casper acknowledged, "but we had not looked at these issues in a systematic way for 25 years." To assess the rigor and coherence of Stanford's undergraduate curriculum, he appointed the Commission on Undergraduate Education—"in the spirit," he explained, "of always asking, 'Can we do things better, or should we do things differently?'"

Based on the commission's proposals, the University established a new Introduction to the Humanities core sequence as the successor to Culture, Ideas, and Values; created a Science, Math and Engineering core for non-science majors; strengthened Stanford's writing and foreign language requirements; introduced minors; and made grading policies more stringent. One of the most significant moves was the creation of Stanford Introductory Studies—small-group seminars for freshmen and sophomores designed to increase classroom contact between senior faculty members and undergraduates. "Students receive a much better education—and an early sense of what the academic enterprise is all about—if they have a chance early on to be in a small-group setting with a senior member of the faculty," Casper explained in 1998. "I do not know of any other research-intensive university," he added later, "that has, in a similarly short period of time, undertaken such an allocation of resources to undergraduate teaching." Casper personally experienced the challenges of small classes when he led two sophomore seminars on constitutionalism, describing them as "the best teaching experience I have ever had." Students, in turn, instructed Casper in the rowdier joys of performing in the annual Gaieties show and cheering courtside at men's basketball games with the Sixth Man Club, a boisterous company of fans.

Funding graduate education was also a priority, especially in those fields in which many students were forced to depend almost entirely on federal research grants for their support. In 1997, to free graduate students from these unreliable sources of income and to support graduate study and research, Casper announced the creation of 100 three-year Stanford Graduate Fellowships, awarded annually on the basis of national competition to students in science and engineering. Casper led a $200 million fund-raising campaign to endow the fellowships, in addition to his active efforts to raise funds for other University endeavors. Between 1992, when Casper became president, and the beginning of 1999, Stanford raised more than $2

Gerhard Casper (second from right) *shares the stage with former Stanford presidents* (from left) *Richard Lyman and Donald Kennedy and Board of Trustees chairman John Friedenrich* (right) *at his presidential inauguration in 1992.*

STANFORD: PORTRAIT OF A UNIVERSITY

billion—over $174 million more than the Centennial Campaign—without a formal fund-raising drive.

Above all, Casper pledged to build on the University's existing academic strengths and seize new opportunities for distinction in teaching, learning, and research. In every area, he asserted in 1992, "we have to work hard...to maintain and achieve as many excel-

Left and above: *New graduates celebrate commencement in Stanford Stadium.*

lences as is at all possible in these times." Stanford's "many excellences" were acknowledged in 1995, when the National Research Council ranked six Stanford programs number one in the country, placed 32 in the top 10, and rated 42 in the top 20.

Faculty members, too, continued to be recognized for extraordinary scholarly achievements. Psychology professor Roger Shephard was awarded the National Medal of Science for his work in cognitive psychology, and five Stanford scholars were added to the University's list of Nobel laureates between 1995 and 1998, including four physics laureates in four successive years. SLAC's Martin Perl won the Nobel Prize for his discovery of the tau lepton particle; physics professor Douglas Osheroff for his work in discovering helium-3's superfluidity; physics professor Steven Chu for developing methods to cool and trap atoms with laser light; and physics professor Robert B. Laughlin for his investigations into quantum mechanics. Graduate School of Business professor emeritus Myron S. Scholes rounded out the list, winning the Nobel Prize for developing a new method to determine the value of derivatives. By the end of 1998, 110 Stanford faculty members had been elected members of the National Academy of

Sciences, 208 had been named to the American Academy of Arts and Sciences, and Stanford was producing more PhDs than any other American private university.

Stanford was also increasingly attracting the nation's most sought-after students. In 1998, nearly 19,000 students applied for 1,600 places in the freshman class. More than half of those admitted brought straight A records from high school, and more than two-thirds had achieved a combined score of 1400 or higher on their SATs. Athletically, too, Stanford University had become the "home of champions." Between 1980 and 1999, Stanford carried off 59 NCAA team championships and 230 individual titles, more than any other university, and in five consecutive years—1995 through 1999—captured the Sears Directors' Cup as the nation's top athletic program. Women's sports earned a record 25 NCAA team titles, and Stanford athletes achieved extraordinary performances in Olympic competitions, scoring 10 gold medals at the 1992 Olympic Games in Barcelona and 16 golds at the 1996 Games in Atlanta.

Throughout the decade, the University also worked to renew its physical infrastructure with help from earthquake repair funds, money from the Centennial Campaign, and major gifts from individual donors. "As measured by expenditures, even adjusted for inflation," Casper remarked in 1996, "we are in the most intense period of construction in the history of Stanford University, including its founding." New construction included the $38.5 million Gates Computer Science Building and the new $110 million Science and Engineering Quad, designed to foster teaching and research links among the science and engineering disciplines; two new graduate student residences; restoration or seismic strengthening of 240 buildings—including the Museum of Art, the west wing of Green Library, and the Inner Quad; and expansion and renovation of the Stanford Medical Center. In 1997, Stanford also merged its hospitals and clinics with those of UC-San Francisco to respond to the pressures of managed care and enhance the financial, educational, research, and clinical strengths of the two academic medical centers.

Preceding pages: *Afternoon shadows on the Inner Quad.* **Left:** *Hoover Tower at sunset.*

In every sense, Casper has said, "we must build Stanford steadfastly, stone by stone," supported by the efforts and energy of students, faculty, staff, graduates, and friends. More than one hundred years after its founding, Stanford University is, as William James predicted, a place "not vast but intense; ...devoted to truth, radiating influence, setting standards." Tempered by adversity and propelled, as David Starr Jordan observed, by "the hunger and thirst after knowledge—that undying curiosity," Stanford continues to explore new frontiers of research and learning, reaching for higher horizons.

CENTERS OF LEARNING AND RESEARCH

Graduate School of Business

THE GRADUATE SCHOOL OF Business was founded in 1925 at the urging of Herbert Hoover, a Stanford alumnus who was then serving as secretary of commerce in the Coolidge administration. Worried that California was losing its most promising management students to business schools in the East, Hoover and 125 of his business associates raised the funds to open the new Graduate School of Business, to be housed in Stanford's Jordan Hall.

By the late 1950s, the school had become known as a regional institution with respected advanced management courses—including the Executive Development Program for senior-level executives, introduced in 1952; and the Stanford Sloan Program for middle managers, initiated in 1957. Then, in 1958, the school began a major transformation

under the leadership of Dean Ernest C. Arbuckle, '33, MBA '36, former executive vice president of W. R. Grace & Co. Led by the energetic new dean, the school attracted major funding from the Ford Foundation, which had identified Stanford, Harvard, Carnegie, Columbia, and Chicago as potential new centers of excellence in management education. The school quickly recruited outstanding new faculty members, raised the caliber of applicants, and for the first time brought the disciplines of sociology, economics, and operations research to bear on business education. From these initial steps, the Stanford Graduate School of Business has earned a reputation for outstanding teaching and research closely linked to the realities of management practice.

Under Dean Robert Jaedicke, during the 1980s, the school added a number of endowed professorships recognizing outstanding faculty and expanded with the opening of the Littlefield Management Center, a three-story office and classroom building. Today, the school is a leader in the quality of its faculty, students, research, and academic offerings. The Business School's 115 faculty members include two Nobel Prize winners, seven members of the

American Academy of Arts and Sciences, and three members of the National Academy of Sciences. It is the most selective business school in the country, choosing each class of 360 MBA candidates from a pool of more than 7,000 applicants. The student body also includes doctoral students and mid-career executives who pursue master's degrees in the nine-month Stanford Sloan Program. In addition, some 700 executives take part in intensive management education programs held during the summer.

Since the 1980s, the Graduate School of Business has worked closely with companies to shape its curriculum and research agenda and to prepare students for evolving business conditions and technologies. The Stanford Project on Emerging Companies takes advantage of the school's location in Silicon Valley to explore how entrepreneurial firms are created, what their common development patterns may be, and how management

Left: *William Sharpe, professor of finance, has developed analytical tools including the Capital Asset Pricing Model, the Sharpe Ratio for investment performance analysis, and the binomial method for the valuation of options. In 1990, he was awarded the Nobel Prize in Economic Sciences.*

decisions affect performance. The Stanford Computer Industry Project, an interdisciplinary research program, focuses on the business, political, and technical aspects of the global information technology industry; and the Stanford Integrated Manufacturing Association, jointly chaired by business and engineering faculty, is a forum for world-class manufacturing research and collaboration.

At the same time, the school is regarded as the leading MBA program in public and nonprofit management. The Public Management Program—founded in 1971 by Arjay Miller, former president of Ford Motor Company and dean of the school from 1969 to 1979—prepares students to lead a wide variety of public and nonprofit organizations. The Global Management Program for MBA students also grants a certificate to students who select courses with an international focus.

The school draws on the intellectual resources of many other academic centers at Stanford, and students may earn joint degrees in such fields as law, engineering, education, international policy studies, East Asian studies, mechanical engineering, and Russian and East European studies. By collaborating with industry leaders and faculty from a wide range of disciplines, the school is enhancing understanding of complex business challenges and bringing emerging issues into the classroom quickly, with a focus on excellence, managerial relevance, and scholarly rigor.

Above: *As a lecturer in the Graduate School of Business, Andrew S. Grove, Intel Corp.'s chairman and chief executive officer, guides business school students in "Strategy and Action in the Information Processing Industry."*
Left: *The central arch of the Edmund W. Littlefield Center, dedicated in 1988, frames the main Business School building.*

School of Earth Sciences

THE SCHOOL OF EARTH Sciences dates back to the earliest days of the University. President David Starr Jordan's first faculty appointment was geologist John Casper Branner, a former Cornell classmate, whom he named chair of Stanford's new Department of Geology. Branner arrived in Palo Alto with two freight cars loaded with his vast library of geological books, pamphlets, and maps—a collection that became the core of the 110,000-volume Branner Earth Sciences Library, one of the most highly regarded collections in the world.

Organized as a school in 1947—encompassing "all subjects having the common denominator of minerals and rocks"—Earth Sciences at Stanford focused, for much of its early history, on geology, mining, petroleum engi-

neering, and the search for and extraction of natural resources. Stanford earth scientists are world leaders in research focusing on the flow and recovery of subsurface water, oil, gas, and geothermal energy.

The school has complemented its expertise in resource recovery with an expanding emphasis on environmental earth science. Researchers have focused especially on the physical and geochemical processes relating to organic and inorganic contaminants in ground water.

Environmental science is the subject of an undergraduate earth systems program, which offers a science-based, interdisciplinary approach to regional and global environmental issues—from the interaction of biological and geological processes to global change and environmental policy.

The school is also a leader in the study of plate tectonics, the unified theory of the evolution and movement of the earth's crust and the basic process that causes earthquakes, volcanic eruptions, and mountain building. In the mid-1960s, Allan V. Cox—who served as dean of the school from 1979 until his death in 1987—conducted experiments with Richard Doell and G. Brent Dalrymple at the United States Geological Survey (USGS) to determine the timing of reversals in the earth's magnetic field. Their work provided the key to understanding sea-floor spreading and continental drift and documenting the movement of the huge "plates" that make up the earth's crust.

Researchers in the school continue to employ new technological tools to advance the understanding of the earth's movement—placing sensors deep in the earth's crust in the San Andreas Fault to detect underlying seismic change and using the global positioning system and radar interferometry to predict eruptions of volcanoes.

In the 1970s and '80s, Stanford

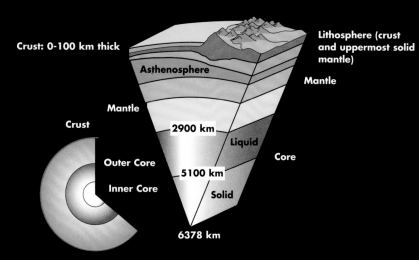

Crust: 0-100 km thick

Lithosphere (crust and uppermost solid mantle)

Asthenosphere

Mantle

Crust

Mantle

2900 km

Liquid

Outer Core

Core

5100 km

Inner Core

Solid

6378 km

Left: Research by Stanford geophysicists has been central to the understanding of plate tectonics, movements of the earth's crust that result in seismic and volcanic activity.

earth scientists pioneered computer and mathematical techniques for imaging the earth's crust and describing the complex rocks created by geologic processes. Researchers have also used Stanford's Synchrotron Radiation Laboratory to study the chemistry of mineral surfaces. Construction of advanced earth sciences laboratories—including a new Center for Ion Probe Analysis, jointly funded by Stanford and the USGS—enable Stanford researchers to conduct important basic research into the physical, chemical, and biological processes that form the materials of the earth, shape the landscape, influence the migration of pollutants, and determine the location of energy resources.

As earth sciences at Stanford move into the 21st century, research is beginning in the study of ocean margins. The geological processes at the boundaries of ocean and continent are keys to identifying and understanding environmental change, climate fluctuations, tectonic activity, and other processes that affect human populations. This emphasis complements the traditional strengths of the School of Earth Sciences at Stanford: geochemistry and geochronology, sedimentary basin structure and evolution, continental dynamics, fluid flow in the subsurface, and environmental earth sciences. The school aims to build the base of science of the earth, both for its own sake and to address the changing needs and environmental challenges of human societies.

Above: *In 1992, geological and environmental sciences professor Elizabeth Miller led a National Science Foundation expedition to explore the land bridge linking Asia and North America across the Bering Strait.*
Left: *Trevor Ireland* (left), *assistant professor of geological and environmental sciences, teams with the U.S. Geological Survey's Joe Wooden to operate the SHRIMP (Sensitive High Resolution Ion MicroProbe). This instrument, purchased jointly by Stanford and the USGS in 1998, can pinpoint the age and precise chemical composition of tiny dust particles from earth and extraterrestrial sources.*

School of Education

T HE SCHOOL OF EDUCATION was one of Stanford's original departments when the University opened in 1891. In 1898, its first chair, Ellwood P. Cubberley, arrived at Stanford and established the department's early leadership in educational research. That reputation was enhanced by the appointment of psychologist Lewis M. Terman to the education faculty in 1910. In 1916, Terman developed the Stanford-Binet IQ scale. Then, in 1921, he launched his famous lifetime study of 1,528 gifted children with IQs above 140, demonstrating that those children as a whole tended to be physically and psychologically healthier than average.

Cubberley, in many ways, built the School of Education structurally and academically. As editor of Houghton Mifflin's Riverside Textbooks in Education for 30 years, he earned income and invested it so astutely that he and his wife were able

to donate a total of $772,000 to the University. Much of their gift financed construction of the School of Education building in 1938 and the purchase of books for its new library.

For the first half of the 20th century, the Stanford School of Education was largely known as a training center for teachers and administrators in the western United States. In the years after World War II, however, faculty members played an active role in educational missions to Latin America, postwar Germany, and the Philippines, and they researched educational systems and strategies for

developing countries. By the mid-1960s, the school had also developed a reputation for applying social science research to basic issues in education. School of Education faculty helped pioneer the "new math" curricular reform of the '60s and helped professionalize teaching by identifying, for the first time, basic cognitive and

Above: *Lewis Terman, who joined the education faculty in 1910, was a pioneer in educational psychology and devised the widely used Stanford-Binet IQ test.* Left: *Recent books by education faculty address timely issues including student and school assessment.*

pedagogical skills that instructors can acquire.

Since then—incorporating disciplines such as anthropology, economics, history, linguistics, philosophy, political science, psychology, and statistics—the School of Education has continued to devise basic and novel approaches to reform, from classroom instruction to the measurement of academic achievement. The school has also paired its emphasis on empirical research with a firm grounding in the everyday world of education practice. In the 1980s for example, the Stanford in the Schools Project established close links between the University and local schools. In classrooms, in state departments of education, and with the federal government, researchers worked with teachers and administrators to solve problems that arise out of everyday education practice. This work continues today as Stanford supports school change through professional development for school practitioners.

Other classroom-based programs include the Middle-School Mathematics Through Applications Project. A collaboration between teachers and the Institute for Research on Learning, the program uses mathematical concepts and computer technology to help solve design problems. The project team conducts related research on teaching and learning and develops curriculum materials, teaching practices, and interactive computer programs used throughout the nation.

A key focus is exposing future educators to the tools they need to be leaders in their profession. The new Learning, Design and Technology Program integrates education with technology and brings to bear the intellectual resources of local educational and corporate institutions, as well as other disciplines at Stanford. The rapid advance of information technologies in teaching—and the potential of new learning environments—are important arenas for ongoing education research.

School of Engineering

EAGER TO PREPARE STUDENTS for "personal success and direct usefulness in life," Leland and Jane Stanford initially considered building a school for civil and mechanical engineering on their grounds in Palo Alto. That notion led to their vision of founding a full-fledged university—one in which engineering, from the beginning, has played a major role.

As early as 1915, Stanford engineers were making important contributions. Before World War I, aeronautical engineering professor William F. Durand was the foremost authority on wind tunnels, and his study of aircraft propellers, completed in 1926, influenced the design of air-planes for more than 20 years.

It was Frederick E. Terman, however, who established the University as a leading center of electronics teaching and research. After earning degrees in chemistry and electrical engineering at Stanford and MIT, Terman returned to Stanford in 1926 as an electrical engineering professor. He fostered a relationship between Stanford engineers and local electronics companies, encouraging young business-oriented graduates—including David Packard and William Hewlett—to start their own electronics firms in the area. After World War II, as dean of the School of Engineering, Terman became even more convinced of the potential synergies between Stanford engineers and industry and envisioned a technology hub centered around the Stanford campus. In the 1950s, the School of Engineering was buoyed by a post-war wave of government-funded research, and Silicon Valley was born as electronics firms, realizing Terman's vision, settled near the University to be close to engineering graduates and leading-edge research.

With nine departments, the School of Engineering is second only to Humanities and Sciences in size, and it is responsible for teaching a

Top: *Integrated circuit from Fairchild Semiconductor Corporation, a Silicon Valley firm that spun off in 1957 from Shockley Transistor Laboratory. William J. Shockley, professor of engineering at Stanford from 1958 to 1975, invented the transistor and received the Nobel Prize for Physics in 1956.*
Left: *In 1996, pioneer electronics entrepreneurs David Packard (left) and William Hewlett met with Microsoft chairman and CEO Bill Gates at the dedication of Stanford's new Gates Computer Science Building.*

quarter of all Stanford students. Its 217 faculty members include one Nobel laureate, six National Medal of Science winners, four recipients of the National Medal of Technology, 16 members of the National Academy of Sciences, 58 members of the National Academy of Engineering, and 28 members of the American Academy of Arts and Sciences. In 1995, a National Research Council study ranked three of the school's departments (computer science, electrical engineering, and mechanical engineering) number-one in the nation and rated five of its other departments in the top 10.

The School of Engineering has produced many pioneers in the development of electronic materials and integrated circuits, computers, lasers, biochemistry, and the Internet. Hewlett and

Packard founded the Hewlett-Packard Company in Palo Alto in 1939. Stanford PhD Marcian E. "Ted" Hoff invented the microprocessor in 1968. Vint Cerf, '65—who taught electrical engineering and computer science at Stanford from 1972 to 1976—is regarded as the "father of the Internet" for co-designing the system in 1973. Jim Clark, a professor of electrical engineering from 1979 to 1985, founded Netscape, one of the first standard interfaces for the World Wide Web. In 1994, Silicon Valley companies created by Stanford faculty members, staff or alumni—including Sun Microsystems, Silicon Graphics, Cisco, and Yahoo!—accounted for $53 billion in revenues, 62 percent of the total generated by Valley firms.

Through the Stanford Center for Professional Development, the school remains a leading source of continuing education for electronics companies, providing live, videotaped and on-line course

sequences that keep working engineers up-to-date on new technology. Collaborating with faculty and students in earth sciences, biological sciences, and the Graduate School of Business, the School of Engineering is laying the groundwork for the next wave of engineering advances in fields as diverse as biotechnology, information science, telecommunications, advanced manufacturing, and materials research.

Above: With a concept and a $15,000 loan from their parents, six Stanford students—three of them computer science majors—launched Excite, a top Internet search-engine firm. Excite's founders are (clockwise from center) Joe Kraus, Ben Lutch, Mark Van Haren, Martin Reinfried, Ryan McIntyre, and Graham Spencer.
Left: *As doctoral students in the School of Engineering, David Filo (left) and Jerry Yang created Yahoo! in 1994 to help fellow students find and keep track of the best web sites.*

School of Humanities and Sciences

SINCE THE EARLIEST DAYS OF the University, the humanities, natural sciences, and social sciences have comprised the core of undergraduate education at Stanford. These diverse disciplines—once housed in the Schools of Biological Sciences, Physical Sciences, Social Sciences, and Humanities—were brought together in 1948 as the School of Humanities and Sciences, the University's largest school. In its fifth decade, Humanities and Sciences continues to be responsible for more than 80 percent of all undergraduate teaching and awards the greatest number of Stanford PhDs. In 1995, 93 percent of its departments were ranked among the top 10 in the country, according to a study by the National Research Council.

Over the years, scholar-teachers in the School of Humanities and Sciences have been recognized worldwide for their research and creative work. For example, author Wallace Stegner, founder of the Stanford Creative Writing Program, was awarded the Pulitzer Prize in 1972 for his novel *Angle of Repose*, and in 1981, physics professor Arthur L. Schawlow won the Nobel Prize for his work in developing the laser. By the end of 1998, the school's approximately 500 faculty members included 11 Nobel laureates, six Pulitzer Prize winners, 11 recipients of the National Medal of Science, three members of the President's Council of Economic Advisors, 17 MacArthur Foundation fellows, 59 elected members of the National Academy of Sciences, and 121 elected members of the American Academy of Arts and Sciences. Undergraduate and graduate students are continually exposed to recent scholarly developments in their fields and are able to pursue their own research projects side by side with the school's distinguished faculty. For example, as part of the Martin Luther King, Jr., Papers Project, students are engaged in

Left: *In a classroom demonstration, laser developer Arthur Schawlow, a Nobel laureate, shows how a flash of light from a ruby laser does no damage to a clear outer balloon while bursting the balloon inside.*

research on the civil rights leader in preparation for a definitive, multi-volume edition of his letters, sermons, speeches, and other writings. In 1997, the University established four new endowed professorships in the humanities and arts to enable humanities departments to appoint the most distinguished scholars in their fields to the school's faculty.

Because so many disciplines reside within Humanities and Sciences, the school has long emphasized interdepartmental research and teaching. The Social Science History Institute, for example, reintegrates history with social science disciplines such as economics, sociology, and political

science. Some 20 percent of Humanities and Sciences majors each year pursue studies in 16 degree-granting interdepartmental programs, including Human Biology, International Relations, American Studies, and Comparative Studies in Race and Ethnicity. In addition, as part of Stanford Introductory Studies, an interdisciplinary course sequence in

the humanities is required of all Stanford freshmen, with a science core program that introduces non-science majors to themes and concepts in physics, psychology, biological sciences, mathematics, and statistics.

Undergraduates are also encouraged to take on advanced work and independent scholarship. In Honors College, an intensive, two-week program, students focus exclusively on the writing of honors theses. In Stanford-in-Washington, an academic program, students combine internships in Congress and government agencies with instruction by Stanford faculty and national policy experts. Through these and other initiatives, the school is enhancing its tradition of innovation and excellence in teaching and research.

The school of Humanities and Sciences includes 28 departments:

Anthropological Sciences	German Studies
Applied Physics	History
Art and Art History	Linguistics
Asian Languages	Mathematics
Biological Sciences	Music
Chemistry	Philosophy
Classics	Physics
Communication	Political Science
Comparative Literature	Psychology
Cultural and Social Anthropology	Religious Studies
	Slavic Languages and Literatures
Drama	Sociology
Economics	Spanish and Portuguese
English	Statistics
French and Italian	

Above: *In 1985, Stanford historian Clayborne Carson was named senior editor and director of the Martin Luther King, Jr., Papers Project, which is publishing a 14-volume edition of the civil rights leader's unpublished manuscripts*

School of Law

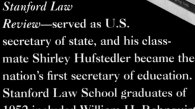

EDUCATION IN THE LAW WAS A cornerstone of Leland Stanford's founding vision for the University. In the late 19th century, most lawyers received little formal training, and Stanford—an attorney who served as governor of California and as a U.S. senator—wanted "the people instructed in the law, for with the law rests the science of government."

When Stanford University's original law department opened its doors in 1893 as a mainly undergraduate division, its faculty of three included Benjamin Harrison, the first former president of the United States to teach at any university. Gradually, the department shifted

its focus to graduate education and was reorganized as the School of Law in 1908. After World War II—when Carl Spaeth, a Yale- and Oxford-educated diplomat, was appointed dean—the school began to build a reputation as one of the nation's premier law schools. Spaeth aggressively recruited top legal faculty, emphasized interdisciplinary studies, and encouraged students to engage in government and international careers. A number of postwar graduates achieved unusual levels of distinction. Warren Christopher, JD '49—the first editor of the

Stanford Law Review—served as U.S. secretary of state, and his classmate Shirley Hufstedler became the nation's first secretary of education. Stanford Law School graduates of 1952 included William H. Rehnquist and Sandra Day O'Connor—classmates who would later serve together as chief justice and associate justice of the United States Supreme Court.

The Law School has continued to strengthen its reputation as one of the nation's most innovative and prestigious legal teaching and research institutions. In the 1970s, it was one of the first law schools to introduce clinical instruction, in which students engage in depositions, trials, and negotiations. The school has also been in the forefront of many emerging legal and policy issues. Students explore new legal frontiers in the electronics, computer, and biological sciences industries through an innovative law and technology curriculum,

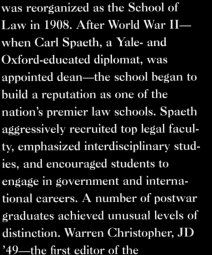

Left: *Former U.S. president and law school professor Benjamin Harrison (seated) with Leland Stanford (left) and Postmaster General John Wanamaker in 1891.*
Above: *Publications of the Stanford School of Law.*

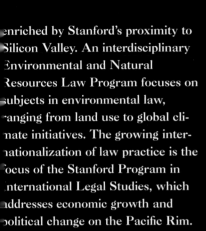

enriched by Stanford's proximity to Silicon Valley. An interdisciplinary Environmental and Natural Resources Law Program focuses on subjects in environmental law, ranging from land use to global climate initiatives. The growing internationalization of law practice is the focus of the Stanford Program in International Legal Studies, which addresses economic growth and political change on the Pacific Rim. A leader in developing alternative forms of dispute resolution, the Law School has also pioneered new methods of teaching professional ethics and the skills of problem solving, decision making, counseling, negotiation, and mediation. Today, Stanford Law School's curriculum prepares graduates for careers in business and public policy in addition to the practice of law.

The Law School's approximately 550 students and 40 faculty members represent a wide range of backgrounds, outlooks, and aspirations. Through small-class and seminar instruction, they explore a curriculum that blends legal theory and practice with a commitment to public service. In the East Palo Alto Community Law Project, for example, students have provided much-needed legal services in the low-income community, working with actual clients under the close supervision of faculty members. The Law School also draws extensively on interdisciplinary ties with the Schools of Business, Earth Sciences, Engineering, and Medicine, as well as other centers of learning and research at Stanford. By transcending the traditional boundaries of legal education, the school provides students with a liberal education in the law and the skills, scholarship, and ethical training to deal with an increasingly complex and challenging profession.

Above: *Justices of the U.S. Supreme Court include two graduates of the Stanford Law School class of 1952— William H. Rehnquist* (center) *and Sandra Day O'Connor* (front row, second from right)—*as well as Stanford University graduates Anthony M Kennedy, '58* (front row, far right) *and Stephen Breyer, '59* (back row, far right).

Left: *Stanford's moot court in session*

School of Medicine

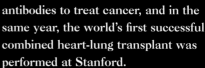

THE SCHOOL OF MEDICINE had its origins in 1908, when Stanford trustees voted to acquire San Francisco's Cooper Medical College—founded in 1858 as the first school of medicine in the West. In 1909, the first class of Stanford medical students began dividing their time between the home campus—where they studied anatomy, physiology, microbiology, and biochemistry—and Stanford Hospital in San Francisco, where they were taught pathology, pharmacology, and clinical practice.

In 1959, the Medical School and hospital moved from San Francisco to a newly completed, 56-acre, $27 million medical center on the Stanford campus. There, led by a team of prominent new faculty members—including Nobel laureates Joshua Lederberg in genetics and Arthur Kornberg in biochemistry—the Medical School soon became a national leader in biomedical research, spurred by new collaborations with the basic sciences and engineering faculty at Stanford.

In 1956, joint research between Stanford physicists and Henry Kaplan, head of the school's Department of Radiology, led to the development of the first linear accelerator for the treatment of cancer in the Western Hemisphere. Since then, Stanford biomedical and clinical breakthroughs have included the first synthesis of biologically active DNA in a test tube and the first adult human heart transplant in the United States, performed by Dr. Norman Shumway in 1968. In 1972, Stanford molecular geneticist Stanley Cohen and Herbert Boyer of UC-San Francisco developed a practical technique for transplanting genes from one species to another, a milestone that led to the development of the biotechnology industry. In 1981, Stanford oncologist Ronald Levy reported the first successful use of man-made monoclonal antibodies to treat cancer, and in the same year, the world's first successful combined heart-lung transplant was performed at Stanford.

The focus of ongoing research at the Stanford Medical School includes gene therapy, transplantation, cardiovascular medicine, the neurosciences,

Above: *Lucile Salter Packard Children's Hospital at Stanford, a teaching hospital, is nationally known for its work in bone marrow transplantation, cardiology, cardiovascular surgery, allergy treatment, pulmonary medicine, and neonatal intensive care.*
Left: *Researchers in the Stanford Sleep Disorders and Research Center, headed by psychiatry and behavioral science professor William Dement, have isolated a gene for narcolepsy in dogs that may speed the discovery of a similar gene in humans.*

sleep disorders, imaging techniques, and work related to the Human Genome Project—an international effort to decipher the complete genetic code and identify the genes that cause inherited disease. The school's approximately 614 faculty members include two Nobel Prize winners, three winners of the National Medal of Science, 24 members of the National Academy of Sciences, and 29 members of the American Academy of Arts and Sciences. They continue to forge close research links with other Stanford schools and departments, including Physics, Engineering, Chemistry, and Computer Science.

The School of Medicine's commitment to excellence in basic research is paired with an emphasis on community practice and improving clinical care. Lifesaving discoveries—such as new approaches to AIDS and cancer treatment—are quickly transferred from the laboratory bench to the patient's bedside. The school's 470 MD candidates take on clerkships at affiliated health care institutions, including Stanford University Hospital and Lucile Salter Packard Children's Hospital. All students, including 280 advanced-degree candidates and 890 postdoctoral scholars each year, are trained to take a scientific approach to medicine and conduct original research, and 30 percent go on to pursue academic careers.

Stanford's medical education, research, and clinical excellence was strengthened by the 1997 merger of the hospitals and clinics of Stanford and UC-San Francisco. This partnership of public and private universities was a response to the changing economics of health care. The financial pressures of managed care particularly affect academic medical centers, which bear the cost of educating physicians and maintaining facilities for advanced medical care. While the two medical schools remain independent, the combined UCSF Stanford Health Care unites the medical practices of about 2,000 full-time faculty physicians. Their combined efforts are distinguished by the integration of research, cutting-edge treatment for patients, and joint projects between two of the best medical schools in the nation.

Above: *The first heart transplant in the United States was performed at Stanford Medical Center in 1968 by Dr. Norman Shumway, now professor emeritus of cardiothoracic surgery. Since then, Shumway's team has devised techniques that have helped to improve the success of heart transplantation surgeries.*

Left: *Since 1984, Stanford's Life Flight helicopters and caregivers have transported more than 500 critically ill and injured patients a year to Stanford Medical Center for treatment.*

Hoover Institution on War, Revolution and Peace

THE CREATION OF THE Hoover Institution on War, Revolution and Peace was conceived by Herbert Hoover in 1914, as World War I was erupting in Europe. At the time, Hoover was organizing famine relief for Belgium. He saw an opportunity to collect documents relating to the war, from political pamphlets and posters to the papers of diplomats and military leaders—primary source material that would explain the causes and consequences of war.

Immediately after the Armistice in 1919, Hoover asked Stanford president Ray Lyman Wilbur to dispatch history professor E. D. Adams to Europe to begin a formal collecting effort, funded by Hoover's personal donation of $50,000. Two years later, when Hoover was spearheading humanitarian relief efforts in Soviet Russia, archivists began gathering materials on Tsarist Russia and the revolutionary and early post-revolutionary years—including the first legal issue of *Pravda*, published in 1917, and the archives of the tsar's secret police.

By 1926, the Hoover War Library was recognized as the largest collection in the world on the political, social, and economic roots and results of World War I. Throughout the next two decades, collecting continued on the rise of Nazism, Fascism, and revolutionary movements around the world. To house the expanding archives, the 285-foot Hoover Tower was completed in 1941. Vigorous collecting efforts during and after World War II resulted in rare archives on Chinese communism, Japan, the Philippines, Indonesia, Pakistan, and the war in Europe. In more recent years, Hoover curators and archivists have gathered campaign leaflets, underground publications, the

Left: *After World War I, Stanford history professor E.D. Adams and his student Ralph Lutz stood with the first shipment of war documents they had collected in Europe for the Hoover archives.*
Above: *Hoover acquired the diary of Nazi propaganda chief Joseph Goebbels in 1946.*

personal papers of world leaders, and other primary materials on subjects ranging from the Korean and Vietnam Wars to labor activities, political conflict in Central America, and the transition to democracy and free-market economies in Russia and eastern Europe.

Hoover, who kept an office in the tower until he died in 1964, remained the major financial contributor to the collection for decades. He regarded the institution as "my major contribution to American life." Its mission, he explained, was in part "to recall the voice of experience against the making of war, and by the study of

these records and their publication, to recall man's endeavors to make and preserve peace, and to sustain for America the safeguards of the American way of life." Today, the Hoover Institution on War, Revolution and Peace—"an independent institution within the frame of Stanford University"—is a leading center for advanced study in domestic and international affairs and the world's largest private archival collection on political, social, and economic change in modern times.

Its holdings include some 1.6 million books and 4,000 archival collections containing more than 50 million items on western Europe, East Asia, Africa and the Middle East, Latin America, North America, and eastern Europe and Russia. Recent additions to Hoover's holdings include microfilmed archives of the Soviet Communist Party from 1898 until the Soviet Union's breakup in 1991. These resources are made available to more than 8,000 researchers a year, including visiting fellows, resident Hoover scholars, and Stanford faculty and students. Hoover fellows, including four Nobel laureates, are among the most respected in their fields of expertise and are typically at the pinnacle of their professional careers. Some of those who have achieved special prominence in both the

academic and public arenas are Martin Anderson, chief domestic policy advisor for President Reagan; Gary S. Becker, winner of the Nobel Prize in economics in 1992; Michael J. Boskin, former chairman of the President's Council of Economic Advisers; Robert Conquest, a leading Sovietologist; economist Milton Friedman, winner of the Nobel Prize in 1976; George P. Shultz, former U.S. secretary of state; physicist Edward Teller; economist and syndicated columnist Thomas Sowell; and William J. Perry, former U.S. secretary of defense. Honorary fellows include President Ronald Reagan, Nobel Prize-winning novelist and historian Alexander Solzhenitsyn, and former British prime minister Margaret Thatcher. These experts explore domestic political and economic issues, such as tax and health care reform, electoral politics, economic growth, and campaign financing, as well as worldwide political and economic challenges that have emerged since the end of the Cold War.

Bibliography

Allen, Peter C. *Stanford: From the Foothills to the Bay.* Stanford: Stanford Alumni Association and Stanford Historical Society, 1984.

Anderson, Bruce. "This Is My Bliss." *Stanford* magazine: March 1992.

————. "A Man of Destiny." *Stanford* magazine: June 1992.

Blakeslee, Sandra. "The Hoover Institution on War, Revolution and Peace." *Stanford* magazine: Fall/Winter 1975.

Boykin, John. "A Ride to Remember." *Stanford* magazine: Spring 1983.

Bromberg, Howard. "Who Stole the President's Wine?" *Stanford* magazine: June 1991.

Butcher, Bernard. "Freedom Summer." *Stanford* magazine: July/August 1996.

Campus Report.

Casper, Gerhard. "Attributes as Goals." *Stanford* magazine: March 1995.

————. "Our Challenge." *Stanford* magazine: March/April 1996.

————. "Challenge of the West." *Stanford* magazine: May/June 1996.

————. "A Key to Learning." *Stanford* magazine: July/August 1996.

————. "A Long-Term Investment." *Stanford* magazine: September/October 1996.

————. "Saying It with Figures." *Stanford* magazine: January/February 1997.

————. "Setting Some Priorities." *Stanford* magazine: March/April 1997.

————. "The 'Vision Thing.'" *Stanford* magazine: May/June 1997.

Cavalli, Gary. *Stanford Sports.* Stanford: Stanford Alumni Association, 1982.

Chang, Gordon H. "We Almost Wept." *Stanford* magazine: November/December 1986.

Clark, George T. *Leland Stanford: War Governor of California.* Stanford: Stanford University Press, 1931.

Clark, Joseph E. "Alma Mater." *Stanford* magazine: Spring 1985.

Crothers, George Edward. *The Educational Ideals of Jane Lathrop Stanford.* California: Daughters of the American Revolution, 1933.

Cuthbertson, Kenneth M. "Notes for a Talk by Kenneth M. Cuthbertson to the Stanford Historical Society." May 27, 1990.

Danelski, David J. "Sandra Day O'Connor: The First Term." *Stanford* magazine: Spring 1983.

Davis, Margo, and Nilan, Roxanne. *The Stanford Album.* Stanford: Stanford University Press, 1989.

Dicker, Laverne Mau. "The San Francisco Earthquake and Fire: Photographs and Manuscripts from the California Historical Society Library." *California History*: Spring 1980.

Elliott, Ellen Coit. *It Happened This Way.* Stanford: Stanford University Press, 1940.

Elliott, Orrin Leslie. *Stanford University: The First Twenty-Five Years.* Stanford: Stanford University Press, 1937.

Hallanan, Blake. "A Million Dollars Here, a Million Dollars There." *Stanford* magazine: June 1992.

Hamilton, Joan. "A Cue from the Past." *Stanford* magazine: September 1994.

Johnston, Theresa. "World Class." *Stanford* magazine: November/December 1996.

Jordan, David Starr. *The Days of a Man, Vol. I.* New York: World Book Company, 1922.

————. *The Days of a Man, Vol. II.* New York: World Book Company, 1922.

Kemp, Polly Wilson. "It Is Lolita Who Is Famous, Not I." *Stanford* magazine: September 1992.

Kennedy, Donald. "Pro Bono Publico." *Stanford* magazine: Summer 1988.

Kiester, Edwin Jr. *Donald B. Tresidder: Stanford's Overlooked Treasure.* Stanford: Stanford Historical Society, 1992.

Leslie, Stuart W. "From Backwater to Powerhouse." *Stanford* magazine: March 1990.

Liebert, Larry. "Years of Hope, Days of Rage." *Stanford* magazine: September 1995.

Lowood, Henry. "From Steeples of Excellence to Silicon Valley: The Story of Varian Associates and Stanford Industrial Park." Stanford University Libraries, 1987.

Manuel, Diane. "Tending a Legacy." *Stanford* magazine: March/April 1996.

―――――. "The Times They Are A-Changin'—Kinda." *Stanford* magazine: December 1993.

McClure, Maggie. "Some Facts Concerning Leland Stanford and His Contemporaries in Placer County." *California Historical Society Quarterly*: April 1923.

Medeiros, Frank A. *The Sterling Years at Stanford: A Study in the Dynamics of Institutional Change.* Stanford: Department of Education, 1979.

Migdol, Gary. *Stanford: Home of Champions.* Champaign, Ill.: Sports Publishing, 1997.

Mirrielees, Edith R. *Stanford: The Story of a University.* New York: G.P. Putnam's Sons, 1959.

Mirrielees, Edith R. and Zelver, Patricia F., eds. *Stanford Mosaic.* Stanford: Stanford University Press, 1962.

Mitchell, J. Pearce. *Stanford University 1916-1941.* Stanford: Board of Trustees of Leland Stanford Junior University, 1958.

Nagel, Gunther. "Boy in a Gilded Age." *California History*: Winter 1978/79.

Nash, George H. *Herbert Hoover and Stanford University.* Stanford: Hoover Institution Press, 1988.

Parini, Jay. *John Steinbeck: A Biography.* London: Heinemann, 1994.

Pease, Otis A. "The Man, the Time, the Risk." *Stanford* magazine: Spring/Summer 1974.

Reese, Jennifer. "A Love Story." *Stanford* magazine: December 1995.

"Remembrance." *Stanford* magazine: Winter 1983.

Rodarmor, William. "A Troubled Tenure." *Stanford* magazine: September 1995.

Ross, Janice. "A Look Back at Stanford Dance." *Stanford* magazine: June 1990.

Sandstone and Tile.

Schalit, Naomi. "Donald Kennedy, President." *Stanford* magazine: Fall 1987.

Simon, Linda. "William James at Stanford." *California History*: Winter 1990/91.

Springen, Karen. "A Legacy of Leadership." *Stanford* magazine: June 1992.

Steinhart, Peter. "The Stanford School of Education: Ahead of the Class." *Stanford* magazine: Fall/Winter 1979.

Tallent, Elizabeth. "The Big X." *Stanford* magazine: March/April 1996.

Taylor, Katherine Ames. *The Story of Stanford.* San Francisco: H.S. Crocker, 1935.

Taylor, Phil. "Hell on Wheels." *Stanford* magazine: March 1994.

The Daily Palo Alto.

The First Year at Stanford. Stanford: Stanford University English Club, 1910.

"The Man for the Times." *Stanford* magazine: Spring/Summer 1980.

The Palo Alto.

"The Revolution Plus Fifteen." *Stanford* magazine: Summer 1986.

The San Francisco Chronicle.

"The Specialty System in the College Curriculum." *The Stanford Quad*, Vol. 1, 1894.

The Stanford Daily.

The Washington Post.

Turner, Paul V. *The Founders and the Architects.* Stanford: Department of Art, 1976.

―――――. "Architecture as Memorial: The Design of Stanford." *Stanford* magazine: Spring/Summer 1975.

Veysey, Laurence R. *The Emergence of the American University.* Chicago: The University of Chicago Press, 1965.

Wenzel, Caroline. "Finding Facts about the Stanfords in the California State Library." *California Historical Society Quarterly*: 1940.

Williams, Tish. "Notes from the Campus Underground." *Stanford* magazine: September 1994.

Wilson, Raymond L. "Leland Stanford: Art Fancies of a Railroad Tycoon." *Stanford* magazine: Fall 1985.

Wise, Christy. "The Home Front." *Stanford* magazine: June 1995.

Wolfe, Susan. *"And Don't Forget When You Leave Why You Came."* Stanford: Stanford Historical Society, 1992.

Yee, Paul. "An Edifice Complex." *Stanford* magazine: December 1993.

Zimmerli, Elizabeth R. *A History of Physical Education for Women at Stanford University and a Survey of the Department of Physical Education for Women in 1943-1944.* Stanford: Department of Education, 1945.

Index

Acknowledgments

This book would never have been possible without the generous and meticulous assistance of University archivist Margaret Kimball, who devoted enormous time and energy to researching photos and artifacts and verifying the accuracy of the text. In addition, Polly Armstrong and the staff at the Special Collections Archives provided exceptional support in researching and expediting materials, as did archivist Elena Danielson at the Hoover Institution. We owe special thanks, as well, to Martin Levin, former chairman of the Association of American Publishers and current counsel at Cowen, Liebowitz & Latman, for his invaluable advice throughout the project. Listed below are many others who contributed their time and expertise to the publication of this book, and to whom we owe our thanks.

Marian Player Adams, Program Coordinator, The Stanford Channel

Peter Allen, University Editor Emeritus, Office of Public Affairs

Eugene A. Bauer, Dean, School of Medicine

Sally Beckham, Assistant to the Dean, School of Humanities and Sciences

Russell A. Berman, Director, Overseas Studies Program

Peter S. Bing, Board of Trustees

Carol L. Boggs, Associate Professor (Teaching), Department of Biological Sciences and Senior Research Associate and Director, Center for Conservation Biology

Paul Brest, Dean, School of Law

Judith P. Cain, Administrative Service Manager, Humanities and Sciences

Gerhard Casper, President, Stanford University

Cathy Castillo, Director, News and Publications, Graduate School of Business

Philippe S. Cohen, Administrative Director, Jasper Ridge Biological Preserve

Bob Cohn, Editor, *Stanford* magazine

Ann Dethlefsen, Director of Communications, School of Law

Carl Djerassi, Professor, Chemistry

Debby Fife, former Editor, *Stanford* magazine

John Ford, Vice President, Office of Development

John Freidenrich, former Chair, Board of Trustees

John Gardner, Consulting Professor, School of Education and former Trustee of Stanford University

Cynthia L. Gori, Director of Stewardship and Communications, School of Earth Sciences

Anne Gould, Tennis Instructor, Department of Athletics

Richard Hudson Gould, Director, Men's Tennis, Department of Athletics

Albert H. Hastorf, former Provost and Professor Emeritus, Psychology

Shelley Hebert, Former Associate Director of University Communications, Director of Business Development, Vice President of Business Affairs and CFO

Marjorie Hildahl, Secretary of the Board, UCSF Stanford Health Care Board of Directors

John Hennessy, Provost

Michele M. Horaney, Public Affairs Manager, Hoover Institution on War, Revolution and Peace

Laurel Joyce, Director of Communications, School of Medicine

David M. Kennedy, Professor, History

Donald Kennedy, University President Emeritus and Professor, Biological Sciences

Judy Lange

Keith Light, Development Officer, Office of Development

Richard Lyman, University President Emeritus; Professor Emeritus, History; and Senior Fellow Emeritus, Hoover Institution on War, Revolution and Peace

Lloyd McGovern, Curator, Stanford Athletic Hall of Fame

Pam McNaughton, Assistant Director, Overseas Studies Program

Alan Michelson, Researcher

Gary Migdol, Assistant Athletic Director, Stanford Athletics

Pat Nicholson, Associate Dean, School of Education

Roxanne Nilan, historian and former University Archivist

Franklin M. Orr, Jr., Dean, School of Earth Sciences

Yae Ozaki, Librarian, Stanford University News Service

Charles G. Palm, Deputy Director, Hoover Institution on War, Revolution and Peace

John Raisian, University Officer, Hoover Institution on War, Revolution and Peace

Thouraya Raiss, Administrative Associate, School of Education

Trudi Reinhardt, Academic Services Coordinator, Overseas Studies Program

Margaret Roland, Assistant to the Dean, School of Engineering

Cindy Romain, Artist

John Rothmann

Kate Ruddon, Acting Director of Communications, School of
Medicine

Arthur Schawlow, Professor Emeritus, Physics

Richard J. Shavelson, Dean, School of Education

Terry Shepard, Director, University Communications

Barbara Shoup, Public Relations Specialist, Stanford University
Sleep Research Center and Sleep Disorders Clinic

John B. Shoven, former Dean, Humanities & Sciences

Michael A. Spence, Dean, Graduate School of Business

Remy Squires, Audio Visual Specialist, Hoover Institution
Archives

Janar Stewart, Photo Researcher

William Stone, President, Stanford Alumni Association

Nancy Strausser, Assistant to the Dean, School of Law

Nora Sweeny, Assistant Director, Alumni Programs, Stanford
Alumni Association

Robert I. Tilling, Chief Scientist, Volcano Hazards Team, U. S.
Geological Survey

Gaby Tovar, Online Coordinator, Stanford Alumni Association

John Wilson, Professor Emeritus, Surgery, School of Medicine

Photo and Artifact Credits

All photographs and artifacts are from Stanford University Archives, except as noted below.

Cover:
Inset photo, Memorial Church from Palm Drive, Rod Searcey

Inside back flap:
Photo of Susan Wels by Mary Pitts
Photo of Tom Walker by Simon Adlam

Opening pages:
p. i, Angel of Grief, Rod Searcey
pp. iv-v, modern aerial view of campus, Rod Searcey
pp. x-xi, Iris & B. Gerald Cantor Center for the Visual Arts, Joel Simon
pp. xii-xiii, rainbow over campus, Rod Searcey
p. xiv, Memorial Church with "Hope" mosaic detail, Art Streiber
p. xvi, bronze statue of the Stanford family, Rod Searcey

Chapter One, The Wind of Freedom:
p. 23, David Starr Jordan, Stanford News Service
p. 28, 1894 Football Team, Hoover
p. 30, Herbert Hoover, Stanford News Service
p. 41, John Casper Branner, Stanford News Service

Chapter Two, Steadying the Course:
p. 50, Russell Milling Company Flour Sack, Hoover Institution Archives
p. 56, Toyon 1930 Winter Formal dance card, courtesy of D. Barker Bates
p. 58, letter to Margaret Gemmel from John Steinbeck, Copyright © 1999 by Elaine A. Steinbeck, reprinted by permission of McIntosh & Otis, Inc.
p. 63, Hoover paper fan and "Hoover for President" placard, Hoover Institution Archives
p. 64, Hoover ribbon badge with picture and elephant pin, Hoover Institution Archives
p. 64, Hoover family in front of Hoover House before 1928 election, Stanford News Service

pp. 64-65, November 1928, election night in front of Hoover House, Hoover Institution Archives
p. 72, signed Vow Boys football, courtesy of Stanford Athletic Hall of Fame

Chapter Three, Steeples of Excellence:
p. 84, *Angle of Repose*, by Wallace Stegner, used by permission of Doubleday, a division of Random House, Inc.
p. 85, J. E. Wallace Sterling with Herbert Hoover, Hoover Institution Archives
p. 88, biological sciences artifacts, Stanford News Service
p. 89, checkerspot butterfly, Edward S. Ross
p. 94, End Station "A", SLAC
pp. 94-95, overhead view of SLAC, SLAC
p. 96, Martin Luther King, Stanford News Service
p. 98, Ken Kesey, Brian Lanker
p. 100, miscellaneous buttons from the 1960s and 1970s, courtesy of Catherine O'Brien

Chapter Four, Higher Horizons:
pp. 102-103, view of campus with Lake Lagunita and Hoover Tower, Joel Simon
p. 108, Western Union telegram and May 4, 1970 *Stanford Daily* headlines, Hoover Institution Archives
p. 109, Pitzer talking with students, Stanford News Service
p. 111, Nobel laureates with the King of Sweden, Stanford News Service
p. 111, Nobel Prize medallion, courtesy of Arthur Schawlow
p. 112, Alexander Solzhenitzen, Stanford News Service
p. 113, birth control pills, courtesy of Carl Djerassi
p. 114, Richard Lyman on bicycle, Stanford News Service
p. 115, Donald Kennedy with students, Leo Holub
p. 116, mid-1960s band, Leo Holub
p. 117, modern band running on field, Rod Searcey
p. 117, dancing Stanford tree, David Madison
p. 117, "The Play," Robert Stinnett
p. 119, Powwow dancer, Rod Searcey
pp. 120-121, Linus Pauling, Leo Holub
p. 121, Arthur Kornberg, Stanford News Service
p. 121, Doug Osheroff and Steven Chu, Rod Searcey
p. 122, "Roble Refugees," Rod Searcey
p. 123, Amy Biehl, Tim Davis
p. 124, professor Tom Byers with students, Mojgan Azimi